# A SEASON TO REMEMBER

**BRISTOL ROVERS
CHAMPIONS AND
CUP FINALISTS**

1989/90

## IAN HADDRELL & MIKE JAY

The History Press

First published 2012

The History Press
The Mill, Brimscombe Port
Stroud, Gloucestershire, GL5 2QG
www.thehistorypress.co.uk

British Library Cataloguing in Publication Data.
A catalogue record for this book is available from the British Library.

ISBN 978 0 7524 6448 0

Typesetting and origination by The History Press
Printed in Great Britain

# CONTENTS

| | | |
|---|---|---|
| | *Foreword* | 6 |
| | *Acknowledgements* | 9 |
| | *Introduction* | 10 |
| 1. | Farewell to Eastville | 12 |
| 2. | The Francis Golden Age | 16 |
| 3. | A Season to Remember | 23 |
| 4. | Wembley | 134 |
| 5. | Brief Stay in Division Two | 144 |
| 6. | 'Ragbag Rovers' Then & Now | 148 |

# FOREWORD

It gives me great pleasure to write a few words about Bristol Rovers' magnificent 1989/90 season. I used the word 'magnificent', but I could easily use the word 'miracle'. The more I look back on what the club achieved during my time there, in such difficult circumstances, the more appropriate I find the word miracle to be. No ground, no training ground, no money, no spirit, no hope – that's what I walked into when I became manager in July 1987. 'Ragbag Rovers', 2/1 on favourites to be relegated, played at non-league Bath City's ground, 12 miles down the M4 from Bristol (where the team had a very poor home record the year before). We trained in Portakabins at Cadbury's Chocolate Factory at Keynsham and many people were saying that, financially, Rovers wouldn't last the season. However, I played for Rovers in 1985/86 at the end of my playing career, and I saw how fanatical their supporters were for their team and club; so much so that the fans got together to pay my wages, so that I could stay on and play for a few more months. You don't forget things like that.

I would like to tell the story of how the team and squad who played during the epic 1989/90 season was built. Having played at the club, I knew most of the players when I returned as manager, and I knew immediately that Gary Penrice, who had been playing as a midfield or wide player for his entire career, should be playing up front. I also recalled that when I was playing for Rovers in a match at Lincoln City, a very big centre forward, whose name I didn't know, had caused our defence all sorts of problems before going off injured. I rang Lincoln City and enquired after the player and was told his name was Devon White. He had left Lincoln City to play non-league football and had gone back to being an electrician. I rang Devon and asked him if he would like to come and play for Bristol Rovers – and Bruno was born.

I also did something I certainly wouldn't advise any manager to do, and that was lend Bristol Rovers £10,000 of my own money to buy a player. Those were really desperate times, especially with the club in so much financial difficulty, and there was a very good chance that I wouldn't see that money again! However, the £10,000 brought in Ian Holloway, a lifelong Gashead, and it was probably the best £10,000 the club ever spent.

Andy Reece was working in a tyre factory when Kenny Hibbitt spotted him playing in a local football match; we asked him in for a trial and subsequently signed him. Geoff Twentyman, Phil Purnell, David Mehew, Ian Alexander and Steve Yates were already at the club, Yates being in the youth team at the time. Ian Alexander was a winger when I arrived as manager, but I didn't see him in that position. I immediately made him into a right-back and 'Jock' took to it like a duck to water. David Mehew was a striker when I came to the club, but again I couldn't see him playing up front. He went out to a non-league side on loan before returning to play on the wide right, where his goal-scoring instincts from his days as a striker were to pay us great dividends. Twentyman and Yates became a solid centre-back pairing, and Purnell gave us pace on the wing. Vaughan Jones was already at Rovers, and having played with Vaughan at Cardiff City, I knew that he was a good talker defensively and felt that he would make a very good captain, which, of course, he did.

You also need a bit of luck as a manager and Vi Harris, the tea lady, gave me a great piece of luck by recommending a young goalkeeper down in darkest Cornwall. I didn't take any notice of Vi's recommendation at first, because we had absolutely no money to spend and we had a decent young goalkeeper in Tim Carter. However, Vi kept on and it got to the stage where she wouldn't make me a cup of tea in the morning – and that's when it got really serious! I promised I would go down to St Blazey to see the 'keeper, who turned out to be Nigel Martyn. I immediately knew, having watched Nigel, that he was a special player. He worked in a warehouse on £100 per week, and when I spoke to him after the game he said he would sign for £120 per week. My board did not want to pay him £120 per week, as they didn't want to sign another goalkeeper, as I feared would be the case. It took an awful amount of persuading to convince the board to take him, and quite a bit of persuading Nigel to eventually sign for £105 per week, £5 per week more that he was earning in the warehouse. Those were the days! It was one of the best deals done in the club's history.

It took some time to get the side organised and adjusted to my way of playing and defending. I believe that when my teams defend, our first line of defence is our strikers, and when we attack, we attack as a team from our goalkeeper forwards. A team mentality, all for one, one for all, play to your strengths, work hard on your weaknesses, want to be winners, be difficult to beat, you *can* achieve anything if you work hard enough, and believe in what you are doing. We ended up the first season, 1987/88, by finishing in 8th position, with a tremendous run-in at the end of the campaign. Not bad for 'Ragbag Rovers', relegation favourites at the start of the season. So, I was optimistic for the 1988/89 season that we could keep it going and was delighted that we didn't have any long-term injuries, as my squad was so small – sixteen players at most. But, I was also worried about keeping Gary Penrice and Nigel Martyn at the club, as both were receiving a lot of interest from other teams after some outstanding performances. We ended up having another very consistent season and finished in 5th position, making the Third Division Play-offs. We reached the play-off final after beating Fulham over two legs and played Port Vale, who had finished 3rd in the league, in a two-legged final. We were leading 1–0 in the first leg at Twerton Park, before a very late Port Vale equaliser, and lost a very competitive return game at Port Vale by 1–0. The players were distraught, most of them in tears; they had worked so hard and had come so close to achieving something that everybody said Rovers couldn't do with a team costing only £10,000, which was win promotion.

This was also a difficult time for me personally. Obviously I was emotionally drained, having come so near to getting Rovers promoted, and so it was time for me to reflect and do some serious thinking about the whole situation. Gary Penrice had played another excellent season and teams were chasing him and, as one can understand, he wanted to leave to better himself. Nigel Martyn was now playing for the England Under-21s and was another player on the brink of departing. My one year contract had expired, and I had the opportunity to talk to Tottenham, West Ham, Portsmouth, Aston Villa and Chelsea. Many friends and acquaintances were telling me that I had taken a team valued at £10,000 as far as I could, and as I was going to lose my better players it was time to move on. I met and spoke to my suitors but then the postcards starting arriving, which had a picture of two Rovers fans on their knees begging me to stay. In the end, 7,000 postcards came to me; they are still in my loft today! As history shows, I decided to stay and desperately tried to keep Gary and Nigel at the club. The club eventually told Gary that if the right amount of money was put on the table for him he could go, but in the meantime to be at his best for the club, which he was.

Now we come to the amazing season that inspired this book, the 1989/90 season. One of the most testing times for me during that incredible season was when the club sold our top goalscorer Gary Penrice to Watford for £500,000, and then Nigel Martyn to Crystal Palace for £1 million (the first £1 million goalkeeper) in the space of one week, when we were *top* of the league. I was *not* happy. I understood the situation with Gary, we had told him he could go if the money was right, but I didn't feel we needed to sell Nigel at that time – I knew that he was only going to get better and better as a goalkeeper. I was also greatly concerned about the effect this double blow would have on the rest of the team, the supporters, and the club, and how I was going to replace them. I was given £70,000 to replace both players, and I received my £10,000 back that I had lent the club to buy Ian Holloway two years previously – with no interest of course! I knew Ron Noades, the Crystal Palace chairman, very well and he agreed to loan me a goalkeeper, Brian Parkin, straight away. In the next 4 games, just as I had predicted, the team struggled to deal with the loss of Nigel and Gary; we lost 2 and drew 2 games, and dropped down the league while I was desperately trying to replace Gary. I went with our youth coach, Des Bulpin, to a Stoke City reserve game to watch Carl Saunders, who was playing right-back for Stoke's reserves. Des asked me why I was looking at a full-back and I said, 'I'm not, he is my centre forward'! I ended up paying all the £70,000 for Carl, and then told him he was playing centre forward for me – and Billy Ocean was born! We also permanently signed Brian Parkin from Crystal Palace, who did a great job in replacing Nigel Martyn.

The whole team were magnificently consistent during that season, never losing at home, and only losing five away from home, and making history by reaching the Leyland Daf final at Wembley for the first time in the club's history. A match we definitely deserved to win, and would have won but for some very dubious refereeing decisions that bug me to this day! There are a few highlights for me: the fantastic night that we gained promotion against our biggest rivals and neighbours, Bristol City, winning 3–0 at Twerton Park; then the following weekend with our trip to Blackpool, where we again won 3–0 to become worthy Champions. The coach trip around Bristol was a truly memorable occasion, as all the streets were lined with ecstatic Gasheads in a sea of blue and white. Lastly for me, was the honour of leading Bristol Rovers out in front of over 30,000 Gasheads at Wembley Stadium for the first time in the club's history, and, in doing so, becoming one of a small number of people who have led out their country at Wembley as a player, and led their team out at Wembley as a manager.

I would just like to mention a number of different people that played major parts in that excellent season and beyond. Roy Dolling and Ray Kendall were Gasheads through and through, and gave a lifetime service to the club; they were excellent during my time there. As were Des Bulpin, Kenny Hibbitt and all my playing staff. I must also mention Jackie Pitt, Bob Twyford, Angela Mann and all the commercial staff. Also squad players who I haven't mentioned like Billy Clark, who the players nicknamed 'Judge', owing to his time spent on the bench, but who did a great job when called upon; and Christian McClean who did a great job covering for Devon White. Then other players like Paul Nixon, Tony Sealy, Bob Bloomer, Gavin Kelly, Ian Willmott, Ian Hazel, Pete Cawley and Marcus Browning. Also, the board of directors, who had a very difficult time keeping the club afloat during some very tough financial years: Denis and Geoff Dunford, Vernon Stokes, Ron Craig, Bob Andrews, and Roy Redman. There were so many people who played a part in that great season, but space and time prevents me from mentioning them all; apologies to anyone I may have missed. Last but by no means least, I want to thank the supporters of Bristol Rovers Football Club, who were instrumental in some of my decision making regarding my career, and who enabled me to have four wonderful seasons at a football club that I will always treasure. Their passion and support certainly helped the club survive some very difficult times.

I hope you enjoy the book.

*Gerry Francis*
Manager, Bristol Rovers FC 1987–1991

# ACKNOWLEDGEMENTS

We would like to thank the following people and companies: *Bristol Evening Post*; Andy Bradley; Bristol Rovers Football Club; Bristol Rovers Supporters' Club; Keith Brookman; Stephen Byrne; Alan Casse; Clevedon Town Football Club; Heather Cook; Bob Coyne; Leigh Edwards; Kevin Fahey; David Foot; Forest Green Rovers FC; Peter Godsiff; Steve Gordos; Phil Greig Photography of Stoke; Jeremy Hicks; Richard Hobson; The *Independent*; Alan Lacock; Richard Latham; Minos Law; Mark Leesdad; Paul Marston; Phil McCheyne Photography of Nailsea; Richard Mitchell; Glenn Moore; Neo Ng; *Nottingham Evening Post*; Robin Perry; 'Sadlad'; Chris Selby; Phil Simpson; Roger Skidmore; Steve Small; Jack Steggles; Stoke City Football Club; Swindon Town Football Club; Chris Tanner; The *Western Daily Press*; Rick Weston; www.greensonscreen.co.uk.

Our grateful thanks are extended once again to Alan Marshall, Bristol Rovers' official photographer from 1973–2006, for allowing us to use images from his vast collection. Every effort has been made to identify the copyright holders of illustrations from published materials. In cases where they have failed to do so, the authors apologise to anyone who has been overlooked and to any photograph owners whose names have been omitted from the above list.

A special thank you to Gerry Francis, Terry Hibbitt, and all the players for their magnificent efforts during the 1989/90 season, as well as their contributions and help in producing this record of a memorable period in the proud history of Bristol Rovers Football Club.

Gerry Francis, recipient of a Barclays Manager of the Month award in 1989/90.

Alan Marshall, Bristol Rovers' official photographer between 1973 and 2004.

# INTRODUCTION

As a child, I lived about a mile from Eastville Stadium. From my house I could see the ground's floodlights above the rooftops, hear the roar of the crowd on match days, and watch the men and boys walking down the road on their way to Rovers' home games. Like many schoolboys of that era, I collected Rovers players' autographs in my scrapbook and watched the likes of Alfie Biggs, Ian Hamilton and Bernard Hall training at the stadium, on the cinders pitch between the ground and Muller Road, or in Eastville Park. Every Saturday teatime during the football season, I would join the small group of football fans waiting at the local newsagents in patient anticipation of the arrival of an *Evening Post* van, which delivered a bundle of *Green 'Uns* (the local Saturday sports paper) to those of us congregated in the nearby corner shop. On reaching home, I became immersed in the day's results and the detailed match report of the Rovers game, which had ended just over an hour before.

I watched my first Rovers match in November 1964, and for the next twenty years was a frequent, although at times irregular, visitor to the north Bristol home of The Pirates. The 'Rovers' Ground' was where I had spent so many (mostly) happy hours watching my footballing heroes, so it came as quite a shock when, in 1986, the news came that they would be leaving their Eastville home of nearly ninety years to move to Bath. But from adversity, the team developed to bring the Third Division Championship and the club's first ever visit to Wembley Stadium. As a youngster, such an event for supporters of a club like Bristol Rovers was unimaginable. The only two opportunities for league clubs to play in a Wembley final were either in the FA Cup final or, after 1966, the League Cup final. And just as every footballer

dreams of playing at the famous stadium, so every supporter dreams of watching his team at Wembley. In 1990 that dream was fulfilled.

On a personal note, as a footballer of somewhat limited talent, who played locally for Bristol St George in the Gloucestershire County League, one of the highlights of my amateur career was playing against Almondsbury Greenway. I scored 2 goals in a 3–3 draw at Twerton Park on 29 April 1982, when the Saints' home ground was unavailable. Little did I know that a few years later, on that very same pitch, a great moment in Rovers' history would unfold.

*Ian Haddrell, 2012*

I was Rovers' programme editor from 1987 until 1991, and thoroughly enjoyed compiling and editing articles submitted by supporters and club officials for the matchday programme, *The Pirate*. It was a challenging time for all at the club, as we were in a difficult financial position after the move from Bristol to Bath. On the playing side, the very real disappointment of missing out on promotion after the narrow 2–1 aggregate defeat by Port Vale in June 1988 in the Third Division Play-offs was a bitter blow. It is not often that a club recovers from the heartbreak of such an event to achieve automatic promotion, but that was what this determined Rovers side did.

A tremendous team spirit had been built up with the nucleus of the side remaining, coached by Gerry Francis and Kenny Hibbitt, and it soon became pretty clear that they really strove to achieve automatic promotion after their narrow play off disappointment. Early signs of a determined squad were there, as an unbeaten run was steadily built up, and while goalscoring was at a premium, the lack of goals conceded was achieved with a determined and resolute defence. Nigel Martyn was emerging as a top-class goalkeeper, destined for a flourishing career in the top flight, while the undoubted class of striker Gary Penrice drew many scouts from other clubs. Many fans thought that the promotion dream would burst after they were both sold before Christmas. However, their replacements Brian Parkin and Carl Saunders ensured the progress of the club was unhindered. With a settled team, which included ever-presents like Vaughan Jones, Geoff Twentyman, Ian Holloway and David Mehew, and with Ian Alexander, Steve Yates, Andy Reece and Devon White missing just a few matches

each, the side developed into a formidable one. For me, the sign of a real promotion-winning team was the number of times Rovers came back to win with late goals, and six consecutive 2–1 victories in March and April; the win at Northampton being a particular highlight. After the remarkable 2nd May victory over arch promotion rivals, Bristol City, the team travelled to Blackpool already having won promotion. To win the Championship in style, with that memorable 3–0 victory at Bloomfield Road was indeed the icing on the cake. This really was a special team – no superstars, but many of them left Rovers to play in the First Division/Premiership. It certainly was a season to remember for fans and players alike.

*Mike Jay, 2012*

# 1

# FAREWELL TO EASTVILLE

Bobby Gould's reappointment as Bristol Rovers' manager in May 1985 was the last major decision made by club directors Martin Flook and Barry Bradshaw. Both men had provided Rovers with loans at crucial times after taking control of the club in the summer of 1981, and had made an approach to buy Ashton Gate when Bristol City almost went to the wall in 1982. However, they both resigned when plans to build a new stadium at Stoke Gifford finally collapsed. Discussions about a multi-sports complex on this site had dragged on for two years, but Rovers had faced considerable opposition from residents, as well as the local authority planners. The decision not to proceed left Rovers with little option but to leave Eastville, their home since 1897, and ground-share with Bath City at the end of the 1985/86 season. The Popplewell Report, delivered in January 1986 in the aftermath of the Bradford City stadium fire and the Heysel Stadium tragedy prior to the 1985 European Cup final, ordered that Twerton Park be incorporated within the stadia covered by the 1975 Safety of Sports Grounds Act. Geoff Dunford and Roy Redman bought up chairman Flook's shareholding in the club and held, at times through 1985/86, three board meetings a week simply to keep the club afloat. Another contributing factor was that the Stadium Company,

Aftermath of the fire that destroyed part of the Eastville Stadium South Stand in August 1980.

owners of Eastville Stadium, had frequently placed injunctions on Rovers playing at Eastville and, on one occasion, this was lifted only on the Friday evening prior to a Saturday fixture.

Not only did Rovers approach the 1985/86 season with new directors and a restored manager in Bobby Gould but, in order to tackle the ever-increasing losses, many of the more experienced players were released due to financial restraints. A squad of considerably younger players reduced the wage bill, but that led to a tougher season on the pitch. Rovers finished the season in 16th place in Division Three. Fifteen of Rovers' 23 home league games were played before crowds of fewer than 4,000 people and these attendance figures fell away as the club recorded just two victories in the final 19 league games of what was, to many supporters, a miserable and forgettable season. In the final home match of the season against Chesterfield, a crowd of only 3,576 saw Trevor Morgan's goal earn a 1–1 draw. Few of those present suspected that this really was a final farewell to what had been Rovers' home for almost ninety years. A moment of history passed by and events over the summer led Rovers towards a decade of exile from the city of Bristol. The immediate effect of Rovers' departure was that a fourth, weekly greyhound meeting could be added to Eastville's schedule, rendering it the busiest greyhound track in the United Kingdom. Twelve acres were sold to a supermarket chain Tesco for £2 million, plus an annual income of £150,000. This left a once-glorious stadium, rated in the mid-1950s as one of the best in the West Country, as a very sorry sight after the Eastville fire in August 1980, exacerbated by the lack of investment and maintenance over the final decade the club played there.

## Eastville Stadium

Eastville Stadium was first owned and used by Bristol Harlequins Rugby Football Club, but in 1896, the directors of Eastville Rovers purchased the 16-acre site which stretched back to the famous 'Thirteen Arches' Great Western Railway line. They paid £150 to buy it from the Smythe family, prosperous local landowners who lived at Ashton Court country house. The Eastville ground then included an old 500-seater stand on the south side, and a small directors' box which boasted cloth-covered seats. Rovers spent a further £1,255 to lay out a football stadium which could hold 20,000 spectators. On Boxing Day 1898, a crowd of 14,897 saw Rovers lose 2–3 to Bristol St George in a Western League match. Much of the finance for developing the ground was provided by the then Rovers' chairman George Humphreys, whose personal ambition was to establish the club in the Football League, which had been formed in 1883. The close proximity of the River Frome, which ran along the entire length of the south side, and the ensuing flooding, meant that matches were often postponed or played in a quagmire. In 1949, the level of the pitch was raised by six inches and extensive drainage was installed, but it was not until 1969 – there had been extensive flooding the previous year – that Bristol City Council completed a flood relief scheme which finally controlled the River Frome.

The early 1900s saw the covering of the standing enclosure on the north side of the ground, and that remained until 1958 when the North Stand was built. What was the Muller Road End consisted of earth banking, until terracing was completed in 1931. This coincided with the reshaping of the ground to accommodate greyhound racing. The football club had resisted several attempts by the Oxford Greyhound Company to stage dog racing at Eastville, but eventually the income which the club would derive from housing a dog track proved too great to ignore. It meant, however, that the arena had to be enlarged into an oval shape and this reduced the ground capacity by some 6,000. The first greyhound meeting took place in 1932, and for the next fifty-five years there were two race meetings each week – without a break. It was the arrival of greyhound racing which eventually shaped the destiny of both Bristol Rovers Football Club and its ground because the racing company eventually became the club's landlord. In 1939, Rovers were £16,000 in debt and although he met with fierce opposition, the then chairman Fred Ashmead agreed to sell Eastville to the greyhound company for £12,000 the following year.

Steve White is thwarted by the Chesterfield defence during Rovers' last ever league fixture at Eastville. Phil Purnell watches from in front of the North Enclosure.

The South Stand was erected in 1924, a predominantly timbered construction that could seat 2,000 spectators, replacing the original stand. In 1935, the betting totaliser, which dominated the stadium at the Stapleton Road end or 'Tote End', as it became known, was built. It was modernised in 1961 when a roof was put on at that end and the terracing was rebuilt. The totaliser was replaced by an illuminated advertising board in 1984. Floodlights were installed at Eastville in September 1959 and were first used for a league game against Ipswich Town. Eastville's capacity was a theoretical 38,000 in those days, but in 1974 it was reduced to 12,500 under the new Sports Ground and Safety Act.

Over the years, Eastville Stadium saw many events; Aston Villa, League Champions and FA Cup holders, were the visitors when the ground was officially opened for association football on 5 April 1897. In the early 1900s, the ground was used for many sporting and community events, like summer charity carnivals. Professional athletics meetings were staged in the 1930s, and from 1944–1948, American servicemen stationed in Bristol played 'gridiron' football at Eastville. In the 1950s and 1960s, crowds of up to 15,000 schoolchildren frequently watched fireworks displays staged by the *Bristol Evening Post*. Regular funfairs and circuses visited the Muller Road end carparks; as did the world-famous basketball team the Harlem Globetrotters in 1965. In 1967, a Sunday market was introduced to the Stapleton Road carpark, and in 1972 a Friday market opened. The Bristol Stadium directors introduced speedway to Eastville in 1977, and for two seasons attracted regular crowds of 8,000. Regretfully, that meant reducing the length of the football pitch, and at 110 x 70 yards it became the smallest playing area in the Football League, along with Halifax and Swansea.

In 1969, the opening of the elevated M32 Parkway motorway impinged on the south-east corner of the ground, and Bristol Rovers therefore had the dubious distinction of playing at the league ground closest to a motorway. Following the South Stand fire in August 1980, the traffic noise from the motorway became even more evident. The fire meant that the South Stand had to be demolished and the whole of that side of the ground was eventually reduced to a restricted terrace. The club's administrative offices and dressing rooms were destroyed and had to be incorporated into the North Stand, which was enlarged and renamed the 'Main Stand'; indeed it was the only stand. The stadium, which staged a cricket benefit match for Gloucestershire and Pakistan batsman, Zaheer Abbas, in 1984 before a disappointingly small crowd of 1,500, saw American football again in 1986. The short-lived Bristol Bombers played 2 games there, attracting 2,000 spectators to their first game on 21 June that year.

## The move to Bath

In May 1986, to save the club an annual cost of £30,000 plus expenses to hire Eastville, Rovers' board of directors took the historic decision to leave the club's spiritual home. A ground-sharing scheme was drawn up with Bath City, whereby Rovers paid £65,000 per year to play home matches at Twerton Park. They negotiated with Bath City for an annual fee of £20,000 plus a percentage of gate receipts. Twerton Park football ground was constructed on recreation land donated in 1909 by Thomas Carr and opened as 'Innox Park' on 26 June 1932. It had been built on the side of a hill on the edge of the city, some 15 miles from the traditional hotbed of Rovers support in east Bristol. Rovers by name, Rovers by nature, it appeared.

It was a revolutionary move, in that a league club was sharing with a non-league side in a different city but, in 1986, it was an integral part of Rovers' immediate survival. Twerton Park was an unlikely setting for league football, with a small wooden grandstand of 780 black and white seats. Rovers' identity was questioned; support was down 25 per cent on the previous season and financial hardships continued, but the club survived. In moving to Bath, Rovers had lost a considerable proportion of the traditional support. There is no doubt that whole generations of Rovers' supporters and their families regretted the departure of the club from the ground that had been their home for nearly ninety years.

Rovers' new 'temporary' home at Twerton Park in Bath – a stay that was to last ten years.

# 2

# THE FRANCIS GOLDEN AGE

Gerry Francis' association with Bristol Rovers began in September 1985 when he signed non-contract forms to play in midfield for an inexperienced Pirates team; the fans clubbing together to help pay his wages each week, because the club could not afford to do so. Francis brought with him a playing experience that was outstanding – over 500 first-team games and 12 international appearances, including 8 as captain – and then ultimately frustrating when plagued by injury problems. Brought to Eastville from Wimbledon by manager Bobby Gould, Francis made his debut against Lincoln City and was a steadying influence that first season as a young Rovers side battled to survive in Division Three. Following Gould's appointment as Rovers' boss in May 1985, his prime task had been to 'streamline' a large experienced playing staff so that Rovers could reduce their debts.

The club were relying more on part-time professionals and an ever-increasing need to use young, inexperienced players. Francis was a fairly regular member of the side during 1985/86, appearing in 28 league games and 7 FA Cup ties, but would barely figure after that as injuries, and his advancing years brought him to a virtual standstill; his only goal for the Pirates came in an FA Cup win at Brentford in November 1985.

Bobby Gould's side opened the 1986/87 season with a 3–0 win at Walsall, and the first home game at Twerton Park resulted in a 1–0 victory over Bolton Wanderers; sending Rovers briefly to the top of Division Three. A crowd of 4,092 saw Trevor Morgan register Rover's first league goal on the new ground from a 17th-minute penalty. However, both the crowd and

Gerry Francis scores Rovers' third goal in the 3–1 First Round FA Cup victory at Brentford – his only goal for the Pirates.

Programme cover from Bristol Rovers first ever league game at Twerton Park against Bolton Wanderers, 30 August 1986.

the result were misleading, as attendances dropped, and Rovers lost seven times at Twerton Park in the league alone. Rovers entered a difficult and frustrating period at the end of 1986/87 season, when 8 home games and 3 away matches had to be squeezed into the final month of a long, tiring season. The Pirates were also in 21st place and faced relegation for the first time since 1962/63. Ultimately, Rovers required 1 point at Newport County to retain their Third Division status and avoid relegation, a mission accomplished when Phil Purnell scored the only goal of the final game of the campaign.

Gerry Francis appeared in only 5 league games and twice as a substitute in the FA Cup during the 1986/87 season. Even at this stage Francis had started coaching; whilst he played for Rovers on a Saturday, he had been helping out Wimbledon manager Dave Bassett by coaching his team's back four and midfield during the week.

In moving to Bath, Rovers had lost a considerable proportion of the traditional support. Rovers' 1986/87 season is one best forgotten; amid poor on-field performances, and before a new generation of supporters could be raised in the new surroundings, the club saw the lowest record of league attendance in their history. The seasonal home average of 3,246 was the lowest the club experienced in the twentieth century. Nonetheless, the first building blocks for the 1989/90 season were being formulated. Central defender Geoff Twentyman, an August 1986 signing from Preston North End, missed only 3 league games, and Gary Penrice missed only 4, while Vaughan Jones, Ian Alexander and Phil Purnell enjoyed protracted spells in the side; seventeen-year-old Steve Yates made his league debut on Shrove Tuesday at Darlington. David Mehew was

Gerry Francis first signed for Bristol Rovers as a player on 7 September 1985.

The Rovers' management team of Gerry Francis and Kenny Hibbitt taking a break from pre-season training, July 1988.

Rovers' top scorer, his tally of 10 league goals giving him 2 more than Trevor Morgan, who joined Bristol City in January.

When Bobby Gould was tempted away in May 1987 to manage Wimbledon, Gerry Francis was appointed Rovers' player-manager in July, turning down a job as first-team coach at Watford to join Rovers and move back into management. His first spell in management, as player-manager at Exeter City, was less than successful; they were relegated under his charge. Driving back down the motorway to his Surrey home after being offered the job at Rovers, Francis wondered, 'What on earth am I getting myself in to, joining a club with no ground and no money?' If he had not been at the club as a player he would not have stayed. He had already confirmed to Dave Bassett that he was going to join Watford, but reflected that, 'There was a feeling about the place and I thought they needed a lift'. He inherited a side boasting the experience of midfielder Kenny Hibbitt and already featuring several key figures in the success to come: Vaughan Jones, David Mehew, Gary Penrice and Phil Purnell, who had all experienced football life at Eastville, as well as Ian Alexander and Geoff Twentyman. During August 1987, three masterstrokes by Francis altered the Rovers side considerably, and paved the way for future success. First, he signed goalkeeper Nigel Martyn on a free transfer from Cornish side St Blazey. Next, Francis paid just £10,000, initially as a loan from himself to the troubled club, to bring Ian Holloway back from Brentford to his home club. Finally, to fill the need for a goalscorer, Devon White arrived a few days into the season from Lincolnshire non-league football to make an immediate impression. They were joined by midfielder Andy Reece, a smart acquisition from Willenhall in the West Midlands.

Three games into the new 1987/88 season, with Rovers sitting on top of the Division Three, the trials and tribulations of the previous season seemed a thing of the past. Rovers won their first 2 home games at Twerton Park by convincing margins, but by February they hovered precariously above the relegation zone. It was the side's away form that produced the greatest concern, whilst Rovers' home form, on the other hand, was reasonably good. Fourteen out of 23 league matches, plus all 3 League Cup and FA Cup ties, were won and Rovers remained unbeaten at 'Fortress Twerton' from mid-December. The 4–0 home victory over league leaders Sunderland in February was the catalyst for Rovers' revival, and March saw the side's first back-to-back wins of the season, and nine victories in the final 14 league matches saw the team rise from 20th to the heady heights of 8th in the table. Francis gave David Mehew a first league start against the Wearsiders in that match and he scored the third goal, Holloway, Penrice and White also hitting the target. Twice, Nigel Martyn kept six consecutive clean sheets as Rovers conceded goals in only one of 13 league matches between March and early May. Francis restricted himself to one further league appearance, in a 3–0 defeat to Aldershot on 1 January 1988, but began to flourish as a manager with the aid of assistant Kenny Hibbitt, a popular and influential figure for eighteen months in Rovers' midfield before suffering a broken leg against Sunderland in February 1988, which effectively ended his playing career.

Making a total of 34 league appearances for the Pirates, Francis' final appearance in blue and white quarters was in the second Gloucestershire FA Senior Cup final of the season on 15 March 1988, a 3–1 defeat at Ashton Gate.

There were two targets when Gerry Francis arrived at Bristol Rovers, as the Pirates were the bookmakers' favourites to be relegated from the Third Division. The first was to stay in Division Three and the second was to balance the books. It proved to be an inspired decision to appoint him, as, under Francis' guidance, there was to be the Third Division championship, a first Wembley appearance and a return of self-belief to the side soon known by elements within the media as 'Ragbag Rovers'. Despite being heralded as a miracle worker by the press, following inspired leadership which took the team to a final position of 8th in Division Three, there was concern at the end of his first campaign that Francis' stay at Rovers might be short-lived. Throughout 1987/88 there was speculation that he might leave the club, as the press linked him with QPR, Chelsea, Sheffield United, Portsmouth and Fulham in various capacities. At the end of the season he was considering three offers of coaching jobs at

Christian McClean; Devon White, David Mehew, Andy Reece, Ian Alexander and Billy Clark pose for an early season photo call.

First Division clubs, as it transpired that he was still not under contract after nearly twelve months at Rovers. However, Francis decided to remain at the club for a number of reasons – but one was particularly important to him. It was the assurance by the board that they would not force him to sell any player that he was anxious to keep. Francis was justifiably proud of what had been achieved after taking charge of Rovers and the last thing he wanted was to see a team so painstakingly built up, torn asunder. Much to the relief of everyone associated with the club, Francis accepted a one year contract on 19 May 1988.

The summer of 1988 saw a further severing of Rovers' association with Bristol when, in August, the club quit their Hambrook Training Centre and moved to the Fry Club Sports Ground at Keynsham. A five-year agreement whereby Rovers paid £11,000 a year to the self-financing Fry Club, who continued to maintain the nine-pitch complex, enabled Rovers to use it on the same basis as Hambrook – the daily headquarters for Gerry Francis and his players. It had cost the club about £40,000 a year to remain at Hambrook, as they sold it for £250,000 in 1986 and leased it back. The annual rent was £20,000 and a similar amount had been spent each year to maintain the site. Because of Rovers' precarious financial situation, the club made the decision to quit the Football Combination after forty years in the competition and to operate with a squad of just sixteen players and no reserve team in the 1988/89 season – a series of mid-week friendlies being organised throughout the season to keep squad players match fit.

Bobby Gould made a pre-season return to Bath when he brought his FA Cup winning Wimbledon side to Twerton Park to play in a benefit match for long-serving groundsman, and former Rovers player, Jackie Pitt. The game, which finished in a 1–1 draw with Devon White's equaliser cancelling out Pete Cawley's 3rd-minute strike for Wimbeldon, provided an opportunity for former playing colleagues of Pitt, including Geoff Bradford and Alfie Biggs, to pose with the FA Challenge Cup. It also allowed Gould to check on goalkeeper Nigel Martyn as a potential replacement for Dave Beasant, who had recently been transferred to Newcastle United for £750,000.

As manager of a club with no money and strictly limited playing resources, Gerry Francis had considerably changed the small squad he inherited from Bobby Gould. Nine players had departed and there were eight new arrivals – dealings which netted the hard up Twerton Park club a profit of £142,500.

Although Simon Stapleton appeared in the opening game, converted winger Ian Alexander recovered from 'swallowing' his tongue in an FA Cup tie against Fisher Athletic to form a strong full-back partnership with captain Vaughan Jones. First Billy Clark and later the consistent Steve Yates, whose wages were paid by the Rovers' President's Club during Rovers' perilous financial situation, appeared alongside the dependable Geoff Twentyman in central defence. Mehew, Holloway, Reece and Purnell continued as the midfield quartet, each contributing a regular supply of goals, with Penrice partnering Devon White up front in a side which was beginning to gel as a unit. With the season only two weeks old, Gerry Francis was already battling to keep Nigel Martyn and Gary Penrice at the club. Penrice's 24 goals in the 1987/88 season had attracted attention from a number of clubs and there were rumours during the summer linking him with Liverpool. If one cog was missing from the success story to come, it was perhaps Devon White's good luck in front of goal. His five league goals were not a fair reflection of his commitment to the side's cause and it was significant that his stand-in, Christian McClean, fared no better at first. White and McClean, both well over 6ft tall, complemented the style of Penrice perfectly, as did latterly loan signing Dennis Bailey from Crystal Palace, who scored in eight of his first 11 league matches for Rovers.

A successful season is perhaps best illustrated by matches played against mid-table Huddersfield Town and divisional champions Wolverhampton Wanderers. Rovers recorded their largest win of the season, 5–1, against the Terriers at the end of October and fought their way to a goalless draw with all-conquering Wolves at Twerton Park on Boxing Day. Once the return fixtures were played, Bailey had arrived on loan from Crystal Palace and he scored twice as Rovers, overturning a half-time deficit, beat Huddersfield 3–2 at Leeds Road. Wolves scored

96 league goals in winning the Championship by an 8-point margin and had scored sixteen times in their previous 4 games at Molineux. Yet, when they visited on Easter Monday, Rovers kept at bay Steve Bull and Andy Mutch, with 30 and 18 league goals respectively already to their names, and became the only club to win at Molineux all season. On-field success, quite naturally, led to an increase in attendances. An average home crowd of 5,259 included an attendance of 8,480 on Boxing Day and 8,676 for the local derby, while over 20,000 watched Rovers' 1-0 victories at Ashton Gate and Molineux. Penrice's goals in both derby games against Bristol City earned 4 points as Rovers repeated, though less dramatically, the New Year exploits of two seasons earlier at Ashton Gate. At Twerton Park, City's Rob Newman saw his well-struck penalty saved by Martyn, who continued to prove his worth in Rovers' goal.

Rovers suffered the humiliation of an FA Cup defeat at Kettering Town after a comfortable win over Fisher Athletic set up an away tie which, after a goalless first half, Rovers lost 2–1. All Rovers had to show for their efforts was an Andy Reece consolation goal after 70 minutes. Kettering featured several experienced players, including Lil Fuccillo and Ernie Moss; nonetheless, it was a demoralising and embarrassing result in front of the BBC *Match of the Day* cameras.

Two second-half Mehew goals and a third in the final minute from White brought Rovers a 3–0 victory over Bristol City in the Gloucestershire FA Cup final, the club's most convincing victory in this tournament since the game against Staple Hill in January 1898.

It speaks volumes for Rovers' consistency that a 5-match winless run and no goals in the final four league games of the season did not prevent the Pirates from reaching the promotion Play-offs. Their rivals in the Play-offs, a system into its third season devised to increase late season mid-table interest, included Fulham and Port Vale, both of whom played Rovers during this last barren run. A second half Penrice goal was all Rovers had to show from a semi-final first leg at Twerton Park, but this slender lead over Fulham was ample. At Craven Cottage four days later, 4 second-half goals earned Rovers a convincing 5–0 aggregate victory. Clark, Holloway, Bailey and Reece all scored against a Fulham side boasting future Rovers midfielders Ronnie Mauge and Justin Skinner.

Rovers were left to face a Port Vale side, managed by former Rovers' striker John Rudge, over two legs for promotion to Division Two. A record Twerton Park crowd of 9,042 saw

Billy Clark heads Rovers' opening goal past Fulham goalkeeper Jim Stannard in the play-off semi-final second leg match at Craven Cottage. Rovers won 4–0.

Penrice score again, as Rovers led 1–0 at half-time in the first leg against a side which had finished 10 points above them in the league. However, Robbie Earle scored a crucial second half equaliser to leave the Pirates with a mountain to climb. In the second leg, which was Rovers' 50th game of the season, Earle, who had scored for Vale in both league fixtures against Francis' side, netted a far-post header in the second half before a crowd of 17,353 – including 5,000 travellers from Bristol – and consigned the Pirates to a further season in Division Three; their bid for promotion shattered at the final hurdle. Nonetheless, the seeds of hope had been sown and they were to come to fruition over the forthcoming twelve months. The thirteen players at Vale Park who came remarkably close to completing what would surely have been the rags-to-riches football achievement of the decade, Martyn, Alexander, Clark, Yates, Jones, Mehew, Holloway, Reece, Purnell, Penrice, White, McClean and Nixon would all feature the following season. However, they would be joined by yet another free acquisition, twenty-year-old bank worker, Ian Willmott, who arrived on non-contract terms after impressing in a trial during a friendly against Taunton Town.

Nigel Martyn once again proved what a crucial figure he was to Rovers' success; promoted sides excepted, no other Third Division side conceded so few league goals. Gary Penrice scored 20 league goals and, alongside ever-presents Martyn and Twentyman, five other players appeared in at least 42 of Rovers' 46 league fixtures. A position in the Division Three play-off final and missing out on promotion by one goal offered, with hindsight, a glimpse of what was to come the following season. In many respects, the promotion push had begun in earnest in March 1988 and Rovers' form through 1988/89 reflected that of the latter stages of 1987/88. But manager Francis put everything into perspective when he said, 'It was a marvellous season, but we didn't win anything.' Rovers' players left Bristol on Friday 8 June for an end-of-season bonus holiday to Majorca, without manager Francis who stayed behind to consider his future with the club, following interest from a number of higher division clubs. Following almost daily talks with director Geoff Dunford, Francis then arrived unexpectedly at the tourist hot-spot of Magaluf to join his players for a few days in the sun.

Rovers players salute the thousands of fans who turned out throughout the Kingswood area of Bristol during the team's open-top bus tour, twenty-four hours after Rovers failed to win their promotion place at Port Vale.

# 3

# A SEASON TO REMEMBER

In early June 1989, Gerry Francis was shortlisted for the manager's job at West Ham United. They were looking for a successor to John Lyall, who was sacked after fifteen years with the club when the East Londoners were relegated to the Second Division. Following his interview, and subsequent discussions with the West Ham board of directors, Francis deliberated, for what seemed like an age to Rovers' fans, before agreeing on a one-year-contract to stay at Twerton Park. Director Geoff Dunford even stayed overnight at Francis' Surrey home, 'between him and the phone so he couldn't change his mind', once the thirty-seven-year old Londoner had agreed at 10.30 p.m. to sign a contract. Francis said that one of the main reasons he wanted to stay as Bristol Rovers' manager was the backing of the fans, 'I couldn't fail to be moved by the near 7,000 postcards and letters that I received asking me to stay.' However, he rejected a two-year deal as he felt that major changes

Bristol Rovers playing staff 1989/90. From left to right, back row: Andy Reece, Paul Nixon, Ian Willmott, Steve Yates, Vaughan Jones, Ian Alexander, Phil Purnell. Middle row: Geoff Twentyman, Christian McClean, Pete Cawley, Nigel Martyn, Devon White, Billy Clark, Ian Hazel, Marcus Browning. Front row: Roy Dolling (Youth Development Officer and physiotherapist), Gary Penrice, David Mehew, Des Bulpin (Youth Coach), Gerry Francis (Manager), Kenny Hibbitt (Assistant manager), Tony Sealy, Ian Holloway, Ray Kendall (Kit manager).

could take place at Rovers in twelve months, and he wanted to see where the club was going in a year's time.

Kenny Hibbitt, his contract up as a player, accepted a new deal to stay as number two to Francis, once the manager had confirmed his commitment to Rovers. He was given the role of monitoring the progress of young players in the re-established reserve team. An all-out recruiting drive to find new talent, largely at West Country level, was initiated by Hibbitt to populate the side, as well as easing the embarrassment of young professionals kicking their heels Saturday after Saturday, with no game to play. After agreeing to remain with Rovers for another twelve months, Francis contacted his estranged captain, Geoff Twentyman, suspended on full pay after missing training to be best man at his brother's wedding – the day before the first play-off semi-final against Fulham. Also fined a week's wages by the club, Rovers' club captain presented a written transfer request, however the Football League ruled that the player could not be fined and suspended for the same offence.

At the end of June, Rovers officially put leading scorer Gary Penrice up for sale, following the player's transfer request, clubs being asked to submit offers in excess of £500,000 for the twenty-five-year-old striker, who had contributed 47 goals in two seasons. He was linked with Liverpool and Glasgow Rangers the previous season, but the only one offer came from Manchester City, who suggested a package that could have been worth £350,000. However, there was no immediate interest and it was almost a month later before First Division Norwich City manager Dave Stringer proposed a £400,000-plus bid.

On 10 July, Swindon Town were refused permission to approach Gerry Francis for their vacant manager's job, ironically the vacancy arising because Swindon's former manager Lou Macari was appointed as West Ham boss; Portsmouth and Tottenham were also interested in talking to the man who had almost achieved promotion for Rovers. Richard Lewis writing in the *Sunday Independent* believed that:

> Personal ambition was expected to tempt him away from the frustrations of Twerton Park. He knows realistically the possibilities of an anti-climatic season and how desperately hard it will be to sustain the impetus at a club where money and resources are short. How wrong could he have been!

Pre-season training started on 18 July, and Wimbledon pair Peter Cawley and Ian Hazel became Rovers' first summer signings, joining their new teammates for training at their Keynsham headquarters. Both players were given free transfers by the Dons and had had previous loan spells with Rovers. Cawley, who first worked with Francis when he was coach at Plough Lane, was borrowed by previous manager Bobby Gould and made 10 appearances in the 1986/87 season, while Hazel played 3 games during a three-month spell at the end of 1987/88. However, the £80,000 offer from Birmingham City to Crystal Palace ruled out any realistic chance of Dennis Bailey returning to Twerton Park. An exploratory operation on Phil Purnell's right knee, the damage caused by a combination of wear and tear and an injury suffered against Bristol City in March, revealed extensive damage to ligaments and both cartilages. But it was decided to rest the knee for two weeks, in the hope that this would bring a great improvement, rather than immediatley operating, which would mean a three-month layoff for the winger. Thus it was basically the same squad as the previous season, considered by some to be an advantage, as from an organisational point of view Rovers could continue to build on what has been created over the past two years. After going so close to winning promotion in the Play-offs, it was suggested that anything short of booking a place in the Second Division would be seen as a failure.

The opening pre-season friendly, on Saturday 22 July, at Weston-super-Mare, saw new signing Ian Hazel score an 85th-minute winner to give Rovers a 2–1 victory after Gary Penrice had put the Pirates ahead on the hour. Keith Coombs equalised for Weston after 70 minutes, following a mix-up in the visitors defence. Billy Clark, who had been a substitute for most of

Rovers players and staff pose during the club's photo call in July at their training ground at Fry's, Keynsham. From left to right, back: Ian Willmott, Ray Kendall, Vaughan Jones, Roy Dolling, Ian Alexander, Des Bulpin, Ian Holloway, Gary Penrice, Gerry Francis, Phil Purnell, Kenny Hibbitt. Front: Andy Reece, Billy Clark, David Mehew.

the 1988/89 season managed to play in the friendly at Weston-super-Mare, but had been troubled by injury towards the end of the previous season and was experiencing pain above his right knee.

Rovers sent a full-strength squad to Sussex to do battle in the Arundel Centenary Cup over the weekend of the 28/29 July. The aim of the tournament was to help raise £20,000 for new floodlights at the Mill Road ground. The competing sides were split into two sections – Arundel, Wimbledon and Worthing were in one, while Brighton, Bristol Rovers and Bognor Regis Town were in the other; the top teams from each section progressing to the semi-finals. Rovers' first game against Brighton, billed as the game of the tournament with both sides fielding full first teams, failed to live up to expectations. The game's best chances fell to Rovers with Devon White hitting the post twice, and 7 minutes after the interval Albion goalkeeper Brian McKenna floored Ian Holloway, who drove the subsequent penalty low to McKenna's left, allowing the 'keeper to make amends for his mistake.

Rovers made no mistake in their second game however, as they brushed aside Bognor Regis Town 4–1. Rovers went ahead in the 5th minute when Dave Mehew slotted the ball through the legs of Rocks' YTS goalkeeper Lee Edwards. Bognor defender John Price put the ball into his own net when under pressure from Mehew after 17 minutes, and 60 seconds later the Pirates went further ahead when the Sussex club failed to clear a free-kick and Andy Reece slammed the ball home from 20 yards. Rovers' boss Gerry Francis even found time to play himself in the second half, and when Gary Penrice tapped in from close range the semi-final place was booked. Bognor did, however, get a consolation goal late in the game when midfielder David Poole scrambled the ball home. Reflecting on his team's performances in the 2 preliminary games, Gerry Francis considered that they had played very well against Brighton and should have scored 4 or 5, but didn't play too well in the second match, but still won.

Captain Vaughan Jones displays Rovers' first trophy of the season, the Arundel Cup, following the defeat of Brighton in the tournament final.

The semi-final on the Sunday against Vauxhall-Opel Division One outfit Worthing kicked off in the morning and the local side took a shock 5th-minute lead when striker Mark Searle headed in off the post. Rovers had to wait until the last minute of the first half before equalising when Devon White laid the ball back for Penrice to hammer home, and until the 89th minute for David Mehew to fire in the winner and take them into the final.

Rovers had already met Brighton earlier in the tournament in a dour goalless draw, but the final match in the Arundel Centenary Cup produced a lot more entertaining football and goals. Rovers went behind after 17 minutes when Nigel Martyn only half-saved a Keith Dublin shot and the unmarked Garry Nelson netted the rebound. Albion went two up after 23 minutes when a Kevin Bremner pass picked out Nelson, who placed the ball wide of Martyn. Rovers hit back a minute later when Geoff Twentyman's long pass found the transfer-listed Gary Penrice. The Albion goalkeeper was caught in no man's land and the striker lobbed into an empty net, but Nelson scrambled in a Dean Wilkins's corner for his hat-trick a few minutes later. However, 2 goals either side of half-time put Rovers level. First, Ian Willmott's cross evaded everyone except Devon White, who scored his first goal of the competition. Then Brighton 'keeper Digweed parried David Mehew's shot into the path of Penrice for the equaliser. Just when the game seemed destined for a penalty shoot-out, Christian McClean, a late substitute for Mehew, headed home Andy Reece's corner 7 minutes from time to put the game beyond the reach of the south-coast club.

On Tuesday 1 August, Rovers' squad left for a mini-tour of north Devon, staying for two nights at Saunton Sands, near Braunton. Gary Penrice took his pre-season goal tally to six by scoring the equaliser in a 1–1 draw at Barnstaple Town on the Tuesday night. Nicky Brooks gave the home side a first half lead, which Penrice cancelled in the 75th minute. The following evening in the second tour match, Rovers got back on the winning trail with a 3–1 victory at Bideford Town. There was an early scare for the visitors when Clitheroe gave Bideford the lead, but Devon White levelled matters before half-time and Rovers gave a much improved performance after the break, Mehew and Holloway adding a goal apiece. Rovers' only casualty was defender Vaughan Jones who suffered a calf strain.

Devon White rises above Bath City defender Tony Ricketts to head Rovers' first goal in their pre-season friendly at Twerton Park.

Rovers' final pre-season game before the 'Gloucester Cup' clash was against their landlords on 5 August, as part of Bath City's centenary celebrations. Following Rovers' success the previous weekend at Arundel, their performance in the first half was disappointing. Rovers' manager Gerry Francis provided a moment of nostalgia for the 862 spectators at Twerton Park as the thirty-seven-year-old displayed the midfield skills that had once graced international and First Division grounds. Francis actually made 2 appearances, Geoff Twentyman went off after 6 minutes for treatment to a cut head, and although the defender came back, he had to retire 15 minutes from the break, allowing Francis, wearing training boots and a shirt without a number, to continue to the end. In the second half it was a much different game as Rovers stamped their authority on play, the transformation starting 5 minutes after the interval when Peter Cawley struck the Bath crossbar with a hard shot. A minute later, Ian Hazel's searching pass from the left found Ian Holloway whose first-time right-wing cross was met by Devon White who outjumped Tony Ricketts to head the opening goal.

Bath had few chances after that, but generally they lacked pace up front and failed to make the most of their openings, whereas Rovers were much nearer the mark with their finishing. Ian Holloway created a panic in the Bath defence when, from a good cross, goalkeeper Jim Preston crashed into defender Ricketts. The ball went out to David Mehew who made no mistake when thumping the ball home from 10 yards. The biggest miss of the hot and humid afternoon came as a former Pirate, Jeff Meacham, shot over the Rovers' bar from a couple of yards out. From a long clearance by Nigel Martyn, the ball reached an unmarked Devon White who made no mistake with a cracking left-foot shot to score number three.

## Tuesday 8 August 1989, Ashton Gate
## Gloucestershire FA Senior Professional Cup final

**Bristol City** 1 – Taylor
**Bristol Rovers** 2 – Willmott, Penrice
Half-time: 1–0
Attendance: 6,153
Referee: Roger Milford (Bristol)
**Bristol City**: Leaning, Llewellyn, Bromage, Wimbleton, Humphries, Rennie, Honor, Newman, Smith, Taylor, Turner. Substitutes: McClaren for Honor (82 mins), Eaton (not used), Gavin (not used), Mardon (not used), Weaver (not used).
**Bristol Rovers**: Martyn, Alexander, Twentyman, Yates, Mehew, Jones, Holloway, Reece, White, Penrice, Willmott. Substitutes: Hazel for Willmott (84 mins), Cawley (not used), McClean (not used).

Transfer-listed Geoff Twentyman was given an opportunity to start the new season as Rovers' first-choice central defender in place of Billy Clark, whose knee injury put him on the long-term injury list. Selected against Bristol City alongside Steve Yates, Twentyman had shown no reaction to the head wound suffered against Bath. Vaughan Jones had also recovered from his injury, a slight calf strain, and Gary Penrice had shrugged off a virus. Future England manager, Steve McClaren, was named as a substitute for the home side and City fans had their first chance to assess newcomers David Rennie, Paul Wimbleton and David Smith, whose transfer fees amounted to £300,000, and they were expecting the Robins to end Rovers' recent domination of Bristol derbies – the Pirates had won three and drawn one of the derby encounters in 1988/89.

City opened brightly in front of a vociferous crowd when Rob Newman had a 15th-minute shot blocked and Wimbleton tested Nigel Martyn with a long-range effort. City's most dangerous moves came from accurate corner-kicks by new signing Dave Smith, and after 21 minutes Turner headed narrowly wide from a cross delivered by Smith to the penalty spot. Rovers signalled their presence with two Devon White efforts, the second forcing Andy Leaning to a hurried save, recovering just in time to foil Mehew. Ian Holloway went on a mazy run into the box in the 32nd minute but was robbed as he was about to shoot. Then Mehew ran on to a Penrice touch at speed and fed Willmott, only for Leaning to make a smart save. Fittingly City's goal, in the dying seconds of the first half, came from a neat corner-kick when Turner flicked on from Smith's centre and Bob Taylor was at the far post to volley home from 2 yards.

Wimbleton's long-range effort went just the wrong side of the Martyn's right-hand post and Smith sent a searing cross-shot just wide early in the second half, but Rovers equalised in the 57th minute. Mehew's cross from the right eluded an uncertain City defence and was just too high for White, but Ian Willmott came in at the far post to thunder a stunning volley past Leaning. Rovers got better as the second half progressed and capitalised as City's new-look side faded. Devon White grazed the bar with a 61st-minute header and Penrice hit a good opportunity wide on the turn. The winner came in the 81st minute, as Twentyman headed on from Holloway's

Ian Alexander shows the Gloucestershire FA Senior Cup to Rovers fans following the 2–1 victory over Bristol City at Ashton Gate.

free-kick, and Mehew forced the ball to Penrice who cracked home a shot from 12 yards. It took a brave save from Leaning to stop Penrice making it 3–1 in the closing seconds.

Penrice proved the scourge of Bristol City once again as Rovers retained the 'Gloucester Cup'; his winner took his sequence of scoring against the Robins to 4 consecutive matches – 3 of those being decisive goals. The match bore far more resemblance to a league derby than a pre-season warm-up, and needed the calm control of Bristol referee Roger Milford to stop it boiling over. Gerry Francis was understandably delighted, feeling content in the knowledge that his settled and well-organised side were ready for the new league campaign.

In another pre-season friendly, on the 10 August, Rovers were held to goalless draw by Yate Town at the Beazer League side's Lodge Road ground. Yate's recent success had been built around a solid back four, and despite Rovers enjoying plenty of possession in the first half, the nearest they came to scoring was when Ian Hazel hit the bar. After the interval Hazel was again in action, forcing an acrobatic save from Yate goalkeeper Mark Sowter, who then did well to pull down and gather a Christian McClean header. A mid-week visit to Chard Town was the final pre-season game, but with injuries to Purnell, Billy Clark, and Paul Nixon, Francis' squad of eighteen registered professionals was already looking decimated as the opening league fixture beckoned.

## Saturday 19 August 1989, Twerton Park

**Bristol Rovers** 1 – Mehew
**Brentford** 0
**Half-time**: 1–0
**Attendance**: 5,835
**Referee**: Jim Rushton (Stoke-on-Trent)
**Bristol Rovers**: Martyn, Alexander, Twentyman, Yates, Jones, Mehew, Holloway, Reece, White, Penrice, Willmott. Substitutes: Cawley (not used), McClean (not used).
**Brentford**: Parks, Buttigieg, Stanislaus, Millen, Evans, Ratcliffe, Jones, May, Godfrey, Blissett, Smillie. Substitutes: Haag for Godfrey (72 mins), Bates (not used).

As the new league season began, the Football League was considering the possibility of staging the finals of the Barclays League Play-offs at Wembley Stadium. The plan was to hold the finals of all three play-off series over the Spring Bank Holiday weekend, with one game on each of three consecutive days. Unbeaten in pre-season friendlies, and with two trophies already won, Gerry Francis selected the same team which beat Bristol City in the Gloucester Cup final to face Brentford in the opening match of the season, with former Weston-super-Mare full-back Ian Willmott named as left-wing replacement for the injured Phil Purnell. Since arriving from Spurs, Brentford's manager Steve Perryman had spent £800,000 building a side he hoped would take Brentford, one of the pre-season promotion favourites, back to the Second Division after thirty-five years' absence. Included in the Bees line-up was experienced defender Keith Millen, a future Bristol City manager.

With only 6 minutes gone in the new campaign, Steve Yates fouled Kevin Godfrey to become one of the season's earliest bookings. Following the Brentford striker back into his own half as he chased the ball, Yates dived in at the striker's ankles and got the ball away, but he couldn't escape the referee's book. After nervy exchanges between the teams, Rovers' defence took over. Vaughan Jones took time to settle in against the early pace of Eddie May, a £165,000 record signing from Hibernian, but Ian Alexander, cool in everything he did, was there to hold the defence, whilst Geoff Twentyman put all his troubles with the club behind him as he marked Gary Blissett out of the game. Devon White became the second Rovers player to enter the referee's book in the first half – four disciplinary points to add to a caution received against Bristol City in the 'Gloucester Cup'. Rovers' winning goal came after 37 minutes when Ian Holloway's left-wing corner was only partially cleared as Twentyman challenged. The ball ran to debutant Willmott whose left-foot curling shot from 12 yards out was stopped on the line

Debutant Ian Willmott fires a shot towards the Brentford goal before Bee's defender Keith Jones can get his tackle in.

by Roger Stanislaus. Five Brentford players fell on it but could only clear to David Mehew who drilled the ball past them into the goal.

Holloway, whose midfield skills were seen more in defence than attack as he helped restrict his former club to a handful of chances, did show one flash of his attacking ability when late on he sent Mehew down the right with a measured pass outside the full-back. Mehew drove his cross with just too much power, but Devon White still got in a good header. Gary Penrice, despite taking up intelligent positions and showing one or two lightening breaks, was a little subdued. But the in-demand striker made one forceful late run and volleyed his only shot of the match too high from 15 yards, demonstrating how dangerous he could be. Only once did Nigel Martyn have to stop a direct shot; Simon Ratcliffe taking advantage of some rare defensive confusion following a corner. Rovers' first-half display was a continuation of the organised simple football which brought them so much joy the previous season; the back four defended calmly, showing innate understanding, while the attack was released by quick, precise passing. Rovers lost their way for periods in the second half, but Gerry Francis still thought it a highly satisfying start against a side that he considered 'could well finish very high in the table'. For the Rovers' manager it was the first time in 7 matches that Brentford had been beaten since he took over.

## Wednesday 23 August 1989, Twerton Park. League Cup First Round first leg

**Bristol Rovers** 1 – Penrice
**Portsmouth** 0
**Half-time**: 1–0
**Attendance**: 4,727
**Referee**: Peter Jones (Loughborough)
**Bristol Rovers**: Martyn, Alexander, Twentyman, Yates, Mehew, Jones, Holloway, Reece, White, Penrice, Willmott. Substitutes: Cawley (not used), Hazel (not used).
**Portsmouth**: Knight, Neill, Beresford, Fillery, Sandford, Ball, Wigley, Chamberlain, Kelly, Connor, Black. Substitutes: Whittingham (not used), Hogg (not used).

On the eve of the League Cup tie with Second Division Portsmouth, it was announced that Rovers had turned down two more offers from Wimbledon manager Bobby Gould for striker Gary Penrice. Gould, who was Rovers' manager when Penrice was signed from Mangotsfield, was looking for a replacement for Terry Gibson, who he had disciplined and placed on the transfer list. Rovers were unchanged for Portsmouth's first ever visit to Twerton Park, whilst the south-coast side included new signing Guy Whittingham from Yeovil Town as a substitute.

Pompey's former England striker Mark Chamberlain went desperately close with a header from a John Beresford cross after 8 minutes, before Rovers snatched the lead 2 minutes later with a piece of clinical finishing from their star goalscorer Penrice. Full-back Ian Alexander delivered a speculative lob, and while the flat-footed Pompey defence hesitated, Penrice raced into the box to coolly stroke the ball past Alan Knight.

Midfielder David Mehew then combined with Alexander on the right and as the defender powered in on goal, it was only a tidy save from Knight with his foot which prevented Rovers from increasing their lead. Devon White and the live-wire Penrice were a constant menace to the Portsmouth defence, who occasionally had to resort to a mixture of crude fouls and desperate tackles to deny them. Frustrating for Rovers was referee Peter Jones's decision to stop play and award a free-kick on the half-way line when Penrice, White and Mehew had all broken clear of a Portsmouth offside trap. But as the half wore on Pompey gained in confidence and all of Rovers' good work could have counted for nothing when Steve Wigley dispossessed White on the right wing, supplied Mike Fillery and the former Chelsea midfielder crashed a thundering drive narrowly wide of Nigel Martyn's left-hand post.

The pattern changed in the second half as Rovers were forced back on the defensive as Portsmouth's players began to show their class, with Fillery and Mark Kelly menacing on the flanks. Pompey's first chance of the half was their best of the match, when stand-in centre forward Chamberlain, deputising for the injured Warren Aspinall, opened up the home side's defence with a clever dummy, but the busy Terry Connor could only find the side-netting with his right-foot shot from 10 yards. Fillery then fired a fiercely struck attempt from the edge of

Gary Penrice scores with a left-foot shot against Portsmouth in the 1–0 League Cup first leg victory.

the penalty area just over Martyn's crossbar in the 62nd minute, before Penrice had a simple chance to increase Rovers' lead. Alexander was once again the provider but with the goal at his mercy, Penrice headed over Knight's bar from 5 yards.

Millwall manager John Docherty and several First Division scouts were at Twerton Park to see Penrice boost his value; his winner was his forty-eighth goal since manager Gerry Francis switched him from midfield to striker two years earlier. Francis expressed some disappointment over the result, as he felt his side could have done better, but admitted that he would have settled for a 1–0 first leg lead before the kick off, as Rovers gained a tenuous lead to take to Fratton Park for the second leg the following Tuesday.

## Saturday 26 August 1989, Field Mill, Mansfield

**Mansfield Town** 0
**Bristol Rovers** 1 – Mehew
**Half-time**: 0–0
**Attendance**: 3,050
**Referee**: Gary Aplin (Kendal)
**Mansfield Town**: Cox, McKernon, Prindiville, Hunt, Foster, Coleman, Lowery, Stringfellow, Leishman, Hathaway, Kearney. Substitutes: Chambers for Prindiville (76 mins), Hodges (not used).
**Bristol Rovers**: Martyn, Alexander, Twentyman, Yates, Mehew, Jones, Holloway, Reece, White, Penrice, Willmott. Substitutes: Hazel for Willmott (87 mins), Cawley (not used).

Gerry Francis was forced to name himself as 14th man – one step away from making the league comeback he had managed to avoid in his two years at Rovers, despite numerous close calls. Injuries to Christian McClean (ankle) and Paul Nixon (thigh), together with the long-term injured duo of Billy Clark and Phil Purnell, left Francis with little alternative. The only remaining fit squad member, not in the thirteen, was Marcus Browning, who had only made the step-up from YTS ranks this season. Mansfield were also forced to make three changes to their side because of injuries.

The best early chance fell to Rovers when neat work by White inside the penalty area released Penrice, whose lobbed cross picked out the unmarked David Mehew, only for the midfielder to head wide of an empty net. In the 24th minute, Cox brilliantly tipped over Devon White's looping header, and Mehew had the ball in the net after 26 minutes, but his firm volley was disallowed after a linesman flagged to indicate that Penrice had impeded the goalkeeper. Nigel Martyn, who excelled with two gigantic punches, only had one difficult save to make from an early 20-yard shot by Tony Lowery. Gary Penrice's inclusion attracted five First Division scouts to Field Mill and he did not disappoint the representatives of Sheffield Wednesday, Spurs, Millwall, Wimbledon and Derby County with a fine all-round display. The busy Penrice and Devon White continually caused problems for the home defence, while at the other end Rovers' full-back Ian Alexander struggled to contain skilful wing-man Ian Hathaway. Rovers' new discovery Ian Willmott had a close range shot charged down, and then White, despite being under pressure, produced a firm header that forced goalkeeper Cox into a fingertip save. Mehew and Reece constantly found space behind the home defence on the right flank, but were unable to make it count before half-time. However, just 2 minutes into the second half Rovers cashed in on their domination down the right-wing. Steve Yates contributed to the goal with a thundering header, cleverly knocked down by the imposing Devon White into Penrice's path. Penrice played the ball behind Mansfield full-back Prindiville and Mehew raced clear to curl the ball over goalkeeper Brian Cox at the near post. The goal stung Mansfield into action and it needed a desperate clearance by Vaughan Jones in the 57th minute to deny Hathaway after the wing man had darted round Alexander, although Rovers seldom looked like conceding their first goal of the season. Fifteen minutes from time, Cox made another fine save when he anticipated a Penrice effort from Ian Willmott's in-swinging corner.

Rovers recorded their first victory at Mansfield since 1938 and remained unbeaten since their 1–0 play-off final defeat at Port Vale in June. Three 1–0 wins in a week underlined again that the side Gerry Francis had built from next-to-nothing had staying power, understanding and a work-rate few clubs in the Third Division would be able to match.

## Tuesday 29 August 1989, Fratton Park, Portsmouth
## League Cup First Round second leg

**Portsmouth** 2 – Fillery, Black
**Bristol Rovers** 0
Half-time: 0–0
Attendance: 5,287
Referee: Philip Don (Hanworth Park)
**Portsmouth**: Knight, Neill, McGuire, Fillery, Sandford, Ball, Wigley, Chamberlain, Kelly, Connor, Black. Substitutes: Whittingham (not used), Kuhl (not used).
**Bristol Rovers**: Martyn, Alexander, Twentyman, Yates, Mehew, Jones, Holloway, Reece, White, Penrice, Willmott. Substitutes: McClean for Penrice (40 mins), Cawley (not used).

The chance of moving into the second round of the 'Littlewoods Cup' for the first time since 1985 was not the only thing on the players mind as they prepared to meet a Portsmouth side who had failed to score in three outings this season. A money- spinning cup run was vital to a club struggling to compete with rivals for wages, let alone transfer cash. This was underlined when Rovers decided they could not afford the former West Bromwich Albion utility player John Trewick, because his wages would have been outside the Rovers pay structure. Rovers were unchanged for the fourth consecutive match, whilst Pompey had midfielder Martin Kuhl available again after suspension.

Andy Reece peppered the Portsmouth goal with a number of efforts from outside the penalty area early in the match. The most dangerous was the first shot on 12 minutes, from a swift move involving Ian Alexander and Ian Holloway. Reece's blast was blocked by goalkeeper Alan Knight, but it fell to Devon White who just failed to hit the target under pressure from two defenders. In the 20th minute, Reece had an easier chance with a lob after Mehew's cross-field pass created the opening, but it was too high. Portsmouth began to look more dangerous midway through the half, when Warren Neill had a shot tipped round the post by Martyn. From the resulting corner Fillery's shot was stopped on the line by Holloway, but there were no other problems for Martyn or a defence in which Twentyman and Yates excelled. A Devon White flick put Gary Penrice away down the left, but Knight got well behind his shot from a narrow angle in the 30th minute. Rovers suffered a major setback in the 35th minute when Penrice went down in agony following Kevin Ball's crunching tackle; he left the field for treatment holding his right ankle. Rovers' prospects looked even bleaker a minute into the second half when Portsmouth went ahead and levelled the aggregate score. Steve Wigley crossed from the left and Mike Fillery, goal-side of his marker, headed low into the corner from 6 yards. Rovers then pushed Mehew up alongside White, and McClean reverted to the right of midfield. In the 65th minute, a run by Ian Willmott gave McClean the chance to cross, but an offside decision was given as Holloway was poised to head for goal. Ten minutes later Pompey went 2–0 up when former England winger Mark Chamberlain seized onto an Ian Alexander backpass and though Martyn held him up and forced him left, he passed inside for Kenny Black to shoot low into the corner of the net. Substitute Christian McClean went desperately close to taking the game to extra time with a fierce far-post header from Willmott's cross in the last minute, but it was well saved by Knight. Consequently Rovers suffered a double blow with yet another early cup exit, 2–1 on aggregate, and a new injury worry for Gary Penrice, taken to hospital in Portsmouth for treatment to his gashed shin and injured ankle.

## Saturday 2 September 1989, Twerton Park

**Bristol Rovers** 3 – Penrice, White, Jones
**Notts County** 2 – Yates, Johnson
**Half-time**: 3–1
**Attendance**: 4,753
**Referee**: Martin Bodenham (East Looe)
**Bristol Rovers**: Martyn, Alexander, Twentyman, Yates, Mehew, Jones, Holloway, Reece, White, Penrice, Willmott. Substitutes: Nixon for Penrice (89 mins), Cawley (not used).
**Notts County**: Cherry, Palmer, Platnauer, Short, Yates, Robinson, Fairclough, O'Riordan, Lund, Stant, Johnson. Substitutes: Draper for O'Riordan (45 mins), McStay for Johnson (75 mins).

The local press considered this match to be between the Third Division's aristocrats, and biggest spenders, Notts County and the section's most impoverished club, Bristol Rovers – the artisans. Despite relying on the previous season's inexpensively acquired squad, Rovers actually started favourites against a club that had gambled exactly £392,500 on winning promotion. One of County's newcomers was former Rovers utility player Nicky Platnauer, a £50,000 arrival from Cardiff City. Two 1–0 wins had given Rovers a flying start to the season, whilst County, a First Division side as recently as 1984, lost their first home game, but won 1–0 at Leyton Orient. Gary Penrice had recovered sufficiently from his ankle injury and tonsillitis to be included in an unchanged Rovers line-up.

The visitors kicked off towards the Bristol end, but inside 40 seconds County were fishing the ball from their net. After Vaughan Jones took a throw-in on the left, Devon White, playing against the team that rejected him as a youngster, won the first of many headers and passed to Penrice, who found himself 6 yards out with half the goal to shoot at.

Andy Reece – from a 25 yard-drive – and White had chances which hit the crossbar, but after 16 minutes the tall striker was on target. Jones curled a free-kick from the left and White timed his run perfectly to place a header just inside Steve Cherry's left-hand post. Eight minutes later Jones was guilty of hesitation as Dean Yates headed County back into the

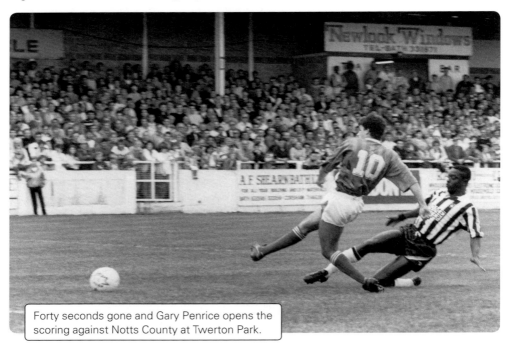

Forty seconds gone and Gary Penrice opens the scoring against Notts County at Twerton Park.

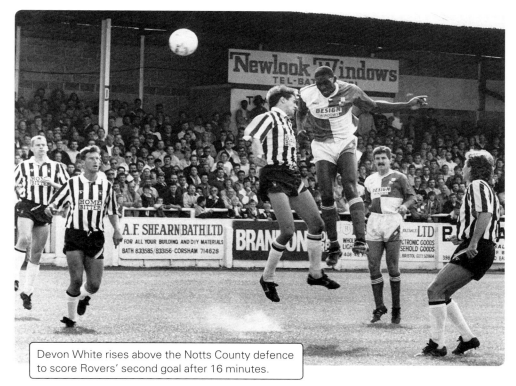

Devon White rises above the Notts County defence
to score Rovers' second goal after 16 minutes.

game from an in-swinging Tommy Johnson corner. After 36 minutes, Vaughan Jones restored Rovers' two-goal advantage with an imaginative free-kick from 35 yards out. Ten yards in from the left touchline, Jones indicated to Geoff Twentyman that the kick was intended for him and then bent the ball straight into the nearside of the goal to beat Cherry, desperately trying to scramble across to reach the shot. Jones then proceeded to celebrate his spectacular strike by performing a somersault. Rovers left the pitch at half-time to rapturous applause. The County manager, Neil Warnock, changed his defensive set up, from the sweeper system utilised in the first 45 minutes, to a more orthodox back four after the interval, the change bringing about a more robust approach from the Magpies. The match became bad tempered after the break and at one time a number of players from both sides were involved in a confrontation.

County were awarded a free-kick 5 yards outside of the Rovers penalty area in the 48th minute for a foul by Twentyman, and Johnson curled a low left foot shot past the wall and the unsighted Martyn to score directly. Despite continued inspiration from Holloway, Reece and Mehew in midfield and the customary command of Twentyman and Steve Yates in defence, Rovers could not manage the cushion of an extra goal. They should have made the result safe, but White blasted over and Mehew had one shot blocked by the advancing goalkeeper and hit another over an open goal. Phil Stant twice went close to earning Notts an unlikely point, but Nigel Martyn's international-class dive stopped him 14 minutes from the end, and then the ex-Hereford man failed to score from an injury-time cross.

Top-of-the-table Rovers' boss, Gerry Francis, praised his team's stunning first-half display, adding that 'we should have scored 10 goals', as, somewhat disappointingly, the high-speed pressure football didn't bring a more convincing victory. Francis, however, was critical of the tactics adopted by Notts County, particularly in the second half, accusing them of intimidation. The Rovers manager was particularly incensed by two incidents when, he alleged, Andy Reece was headbutted by defender Charlie Palmer, and Ian Willmott was also butted; he was especially angry about a high challenge on Nigel Martyn.

## Saturday 9 September 1989, Burnden Park, Bolton

**Bolton Wanderers** 1– Reeves
**Bristol Rovers** 0
**Half-time**: 0–0
**Attendance**: 5,913
**Referee**: Keren Barratt (Coventry)
**Bolton Wanderers**: Rose, Brown, Cowdrill, Savage, Crombie, Winstanley, Storer, Thompson, Reeves, Philliskirk, Darby. Substitutes: Jeffrey for Reeves (85 mins), Henshaw (not used).
**Bristol Rovers**: Martyn, Alexander, Twentyman, Yates, Mehew, Jones, Holloway, Reece, White, Penrice, Willmott. Substitutes: Nixon for Penrice (78 mins), Cawley (not used).

Gerry Francis was able to name an unchanged Rovers side for the sixth consecutive match of the season. Nigel Martyn was back to league action following his mid-week selection for the England Under-21 team in their 1–0 European Championship qualifier defeat in Sweden. Under the guidance of former Liverpool legend Phil Neal, the once-mighty Bolton Wanderers had been promoted from the Fourth Division in 1987/88, along with Cardiff City and Wolverhampton Wanderers.

Rovers were unfortunate not to take the lead in the 33rd minute, when, from an Ian Alexander centre, Devon White rose at the far post and sent a perfect downwards header spearing past the left hand of goalkeeper, Kevin Rose. Luckily for Bolton the ball passed the post with the goalkeeper beaten. Early in the second half, White was booked by the referee for challenging goalkeeper Rose, and then Bolton's captain Phil Brown was also cautioned for a push on the Rovers striker. Then Rovers' 'keeper Martyn, maintaining his international form, produced a wonder save to prevent Julian Darby getting in a shot when a Bolton goal seemed certain. Geoff Twentyman thought that he had opened the scoring for the Pirates in the 67th minute of a wind-spoilt game. From a free-kick to the far post, taken by Vaughan Jones on the left, the central defender headed goalwards, only to see goalkeeper Kevin Rose knock the ball into the side-netting, and then frustratingly for Rovers the referee awarded Bolton a goal-kick rather than a Rovers corner. A badly out-of-touch Gary Penrice shot over shortly afterwards. Bolton's winner came from former Sheffield Wednesday striker David Reeves in the 75th minute, with a 12-yard drive that beat the unprotected Martyn, who had previously made some crucial saves. There was a suspicion of handball when Tony Philliskirk hammered the ball at goal, only to see it strike Reeves, who turned quickly to fire it into the net, but the referee ignored Rovers' appeals that the scorer had controlled the ball with his hand. Reeves, before he was substituted, had an opportunity to add to his tally when he shot through a ruck of players but his effort was saved. Rovers had a chance to salvage a point in the last minute when David Mehew had a great chance to equalise after breaking away from the Bolton defence, but he snatched his shot wide of the goal from a good position.

Francis was disappointed with the performance of Gary Penrice and brought him off in the closing minutes, although appreciative that the player had not trained for over a week and was racked with the worry of trying to decide his future, after turning down a £500,000 move to Wimbledon. Although losing their 100 per cent league record, Rovers were always dangerous on the counter-attack, whilst restricting the home team to a few chances. However, Bolton always looked the more likely side to break the deadlock. Bolton's victory gave them a run of 20 league games undefeated, which shattered a record that had stood for fifty-five years. Bolton's president, the legendary former England centre forward Nat Lofthouse, agreed the game was no classic but saw enough to believe that both sides would be a force in the division, commenting: 'I expect to see us and Rovers among the leading pack when it counts most next spring.'

## Saturday 16 September 1989, Twerton Park

**Bristol Rovers** 3 – Twentyman, Penrice, White
**Preston North End** 0
Half-time: 3–0
Attendance: 4,350
Referee: Keith Cooper (Pontypridd)
**Bristol Rovers**: Martyn, Alexander, Twentyman, Yates, Mehew, Jones, Holloway, Reece, White, Penrice, Willmott. Substitutes: Sealy for Reece (54 mins), Cawley (not used).
**Preston North End**: Kelly, Williams, Swann, Wrightson, Scully, Hughes, Mooney, Ellis, Joyce, Shaw, Bogie. Substitutes: Atkins for Wrightson (54 mins), Rathbone for Swann (78 mins).

With the uncommon luxury of competition for places in the Rovers squad, boosted by the arrival of Tony Sealy, Francis decided not to tell the players who was in the side until 45 minutes before kick-off. Despite impressing in the 2–1 South West Counties defeat by Bristol City at Keynsham on the Wednesday night, Sealy, the former Crystal Palace, QPR and Brentford striker, seemed likely to start on the bench. Francis believed that all his players should know the team system and Sealy had only had one reserve game and a training session behind him. Preston, third from bottom with only 1 point from 4 matches, had conceded 19 goals, yet their twenty-two-year-old former Stoke City striker Graham Shaw was one of the leading scorers in the division with 6 goals.

Devon White, David Mehew and Ian Holloway had already gone close with headers and Ian Willmott with a shot when Geoff Twentyman gave Rovers a 14th-minute lead. He finished off Holloway's long free-kick with a far-post header after Penrice and then Mehew had nodded on to where he stood unmarked. The big defender later described the goal as, 'one of the sweetest moments in my career to score against my old club for the first time'.

Twentyman was involved in the second goal too, after 20 minutes. Another set-piece, this time from Vaughan Jones' long range free-kick, White won the header, and then Twentyman

Geoff Twentyman heads the opening goal against his former club Preston North End and Rovers are on their way to the top of Division Three.

Gary Penrice takes advantage of untidy Preston defending to slide home Rovers' second goal past goalkeeper Alan Kelly, with Ian Willmott in support.

headed it down to Penrice who slid the ball past goalkeeper Alan Kelly's challenge with the sharp finishing touch that was his hallmark. It was his 49th goal in just over two seasons. In the 31st minute, Rovers increased their lead further when Devon White powered in the third goal after his first shot had been blocked by the sprawling Alan Kelly. As a left-wing cross from Vaughan Jones reached White he fired off a shot, which came back off the 'keeper's left leg and the second time he made no mistake. North End came out of their bunkers for a couple of raids late in the half – Warren Joyce firing wide and Mooney just failing to reach a Tony Ellis shot – but Rovers resumed the bombardment.

Preston reorganised at half-time and by changing their style came more into the game. Rovers brought on Tony Sealy for an earlier than expected debut, as Andy Reece departed with a cut beneath his left eye that required three stitches and as a result, Rovers lost a bit of their pattern. Making an immediate impression, Sealy glided past numerous defenders on the right flank, but was let down by his final pass. Chances kept coming for Rovers, particularly for Devon White, but goalkeeper Kelly, who made two remarkable second half stops, and Pat Scully, who cleared a goal-bound header over the bar when a score seemed inevitable, stopped the big striker from adding to his tally. White was also involved in defensive duties, energetically defending in his own penalty area, where he saved two second-half goal attempts with a header and tackle as Preston enjoyed a mini-revival. But Rovers were too far in front to be shaken, although Gary Swann went close, hitting the crossbar.

Whilst praising his team's performance, 'Some of the one-touch football was of the highest quality, built around hard work on the training ground', Gerry Francis was less complimentary about the attitude of some of the fans when Rovers failed to add to their first half-hour goal fest. However, newcomer Tony Sealy, making a modest contribution playing out of position on the right wing, was suitably impressed by the organisation and the ability of his new teammates, describing his new side's display as exciting. The encouraging start to the season and the emphatic win against Preston saw Rovers at the top of Third Division for the first time since 29 August 1987 and left Bristol football fans eagerly awaiting the first league derby game of the season.

## 16 SEPTEMBER 1989

|                  | P | W | D | L | F  | A | Pts |
|------------------|---|---|---|---|----|---|-----|
| BRISTOL ROVERS   | 5 | 4 | 0 | 1 | 8  | 3 | 12  |
| Bury             | 5 | 3 | 2 | 0 | 10 | 5 | 11  |
| Huddersfield Town| 5 | 3 | 2 | 0 | 9  | 6 | 11  |
| Rotherham United | 5 | 3 | 1 | 1 | 10 | 5 | 10  |
| Shrewsbury Town  | 5 | 3 | 1 | 1 | 11 | 7 | 10  |
| Bristol City     | 5 | 3 | 1 | 1 | 7  | 3 | 10  |
| Fulham           | 5 | 3 | 1 | 1 | 7  | 4 | 10  |

## Saturday 23 September 1989. Ashton Gate, Bristol

Bristol City 0
Bristol Rovers 0
Half-time: 0–0
Attendance: 17,432
Referee: John Deakin (Llantwit Major)
**Bristol City**: Leaning, Llewellyn, Bromage, Wimbleton, Pender, Rennie, Shelton, Newman, Taylor, Smith, Turner. Substitutes: Mardon for Bromage (6 mins), Gavin for Smith (62 mins).
**Bristol Rovers**: Martyn, Alexander, Twentyman, Yates, Mehew, Jones, Holloway, Reece, White, Penrice, Willmott. Substitutes: Cawley (not used), Sealy (not used).

Rovers and City prepared for the Bristol derby at Ashton Gate by spying on each other. Rovers sent youth coach Des Bulpin to Ninian Park to see the Robins' 3–0 win over Cardiff City, while City were represented by scouts Jock Rae and Mike Gibson at Twerton Park when Preston were demolished by a similar score. Gerry Francis selected an unchanged team for the sixth successive league game, whilst City retained the side that won in Wales. The game was being touted as the most important Bristol clash for years, due to their respective league positions – Rovers 2nd and City 7th – and the fact that both teams were in good form.

Rovers' first chance fell to Gary Penrice in only the 2nd minute after a poor City free-kick allowed Rovers to build a swift break. Andy Llewellyn misjudged an Andy Reece through ball to allow Penrice clear, but the striker, who made a habit of scoring in derby games, lacked his normal decisive finishing and Andy Leaning made a sprawling save at the edge of the penalty area. City suffered a set back 4 minutes later when Russell Bromage limped off with a hamstring injury to be replaced by Paul Mardon in an unfamiliar right-back role, with Llewellyn switching to the left side of defence. But it was Rovers who were pinned back. Pender volleyed wide, and on the half-hour Bob Taylor hooked a first-time shot against the crossbar and over after David Rennie's free-kick had been cleverly laid off via former Rover Robbie Turner's chest. City winger David Smith reacted angrily to a second scything challenge (the first after 12 minutes) from Ian Alexander after 32 minutes and both players were cautioned by the referee. Shortly afterwards, the incensed Rovers full-back petulantly kicked the ball away as a free-kick was awarded against Steve Yates for a push on Taylor, and he was sent off by referee John Deakin for a second bookable offence. City's Gary Shelton was next in the book for a late tackle on Yates immediately after the restart. City held the edge for most of a physical first half littered with twenty-seven free-kicks, which included twenty against Rovers.

Alexander's departure saw Vaughan Jones switch to right-back, with Ian Willmott dropping into defence and Penrice adopting a wider role in attack. With Pender combating the aerial threat of Devon White, Rovers found it difficult to mount meaningful attacks, but in defence, however, they were strong and decisive. For all City's possession their only worthwhile effort was a Wimbleton header, held just under the bar by Nigel Martyn at the end of a flowing move involving a storming run from Newman and a Shelton cross.

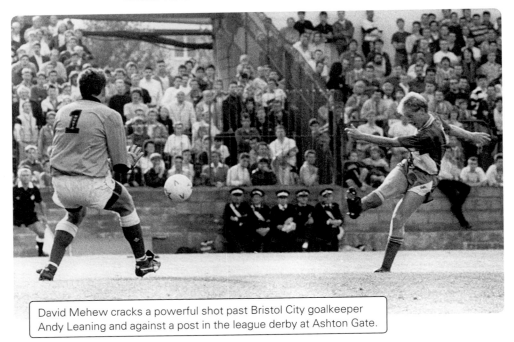

David Mehew cracks a powerful shot past Bristol City goalkeeper Andy Leaning and against a post in the league derby at Ashton Gate.

After the interval, and a few soothing words from both managers, Rovers did not pack their defence and midfield – the usual ploy of teams operating under reduced circumstances – and for most of the second half employed a 4-2-3 formation, creating almost all the scoring opportunities. David Mehew twice went close to scoring, but his far-post header from a Penrice cross was thwarted by a diving save from Leaning. He then volleyed against the outside of a post, while Penrice saw the fiercest shot of the match rise fractionally too high,

Bristol City's defence clears the ball under pressure from David Mehew in the 0–0 draw.

after seizing on a John Pender clearance. Andy Reece scooped a first-time shot over the bar in the 63rd minute and 10 minutes from the end it was White who almost snatched all 3 points, when he lunged to meet Mehew's early cross, but he sent his shot just the wrong side of the post. City's chances were less clear cut as they hit too many, usually inaccurate, long balls at the Rovers' defence. Yates whipped the ball away from Taylor before he could pounce on Shelton's through ball and Turner just missed contacting with Wimbleton's left-wing cross. Right at the end, it required an intervening tackle from the impressive Yates to prevent substitute Mark Gavin, on for Smith, from grabbing a last gasp winner.

Consequently Rovers, who cost the princely sum of £10,000 to assemble, held their line with little difficulty against a team costing sixty times as much and would have maintained their sole tenure of the Third Division top spot if Devon White and David Mehew had been a fraction more accurate. Gerry Francis was disappointed at seeing his careful pre-match planning fall apart with the sending off of Alexander, but praised his side's ability to overcome the disadvantage. 'Our organisation and tactics were excellent in the second half, but it has taken two years to instil that sort of discipline and tactical awareness', the manager commented. Rovers were undefeated in league derbies since March 1986 and sat 2nd in the table after 6 games – 4 places above their local rivals.

## Tuesday 26 September 1989, Brisbane Road, Leyton

Leyton Orient 0
Bristol Rovers 1 – Mehew
Half-time: 0–1
Attendance: 4,675
Referee: Michael Bailey (Cambridge)
Leyton Orient: Heald, Baker, Smalley, Sitton, Dickenson, Hales, Howard, Castle, Carter, Harvey, Cooper. Substitutes: Hull for Hales (45 mins), Ward (not used).
Bristol Rovers: Martyn, Alexander, Twentyman, Yates, Mehew, Jones, Holloway, Reece, White, Penrice, Willmott. Substitutes: Cawley (not used), Sealy (not used).

Following Saturday's goalless draw, the top of the Third Division beckoned for both Bristol clubs prior to their midweek fixtures. Rovers could regain the leadership by winning at Leyton Orient – providing neighbours City prevented Shrewsbury taking 3 points at Ashton Gate – and a victory for Joe Jordan's team could conceivably take them to the top spot if Rovers faltered and other results went their way. A real concern for Rovers was the fitness of goalkeeper Nigel Martyn, troubled with strained knee ligaments, but as he was Rovers' only professional 'keeper he was selected in an unchanged side.

Early in the game Martyn, who was clearly uncomfortable, bent backwards to tip Steve Castle's header over the crossbar. After a quiet start to the match, Rovers came to life in the final 15 minutes of the first half, but Devon White couldn't direct his shot after striking partner Penrice laid the ball into his path. Moments later, David Mehew almost opened the scoring when he struck a fierce volley from 20 yards which was brilliantly turned round the post by goalkeeper Paul Heald. However, Heald had no chance in the 42nd minute when Mehew rose above the Orient defence to meet Holloway's cross from the right wing, heading the ball down and into the corner of the net to the delight of a large and vocal band of Rovers' supporters. It was Mehew's third goal of the season. Twice in the moments remaining before the interval Orient went close to equalising. Firstly, Martyn turned away Mark Cooper's low drive for a corner, and then there was a rare mistake by the Rovers goalkeeper as he dropped Castle's shot, which allowed Danny Carter a close-range shot. Ian Alexander, who had a fine game throughout, then made a spectacular goal line clearance to maintain Rovers' advantage. Steve Yates was shown the red card in the 65th minute after winning the ball in a tackle on Orient's substitute Alan Hull, who injected more life in the home attack after replacing

Kevin Hales at the start of the second half. The challenge was high, but it seemed likely that Yates would only collect a booking like colleagues Penrice, Jones and White before him, and seemed stunned when referee Mike Bailey sent him off, as it was his first foul of the game and appeared to only warrant a booking. Rovers had to drop back when Yates was dismissed, and were forced to fight a rearguard action for the remainder of the game, with Jones switching to the centre of the defence and Ian Willmott again finding himself moved from the wing to his original position of left-back. But Penrice and White still looked dangerous on the break, and Orient had another escape when their captain, former Chelsea defender John Sitton, steered a careless backpass wide of goalkeeper Heald which trickled along the goal line before being scrambled to safety.

Rovers held on to their one goal lead for the last 25 minutes with ten men and deserved their victory. They demonstrated that the sprit and understanding bred into the team by Gerry Francis had enabled the Pirates to overcome the loss of a sent-off player. Victory was all the more creditable because it was achieved by a team with a goalkeeper seriously hampered by injury, and with City beating Shrewsbury Town the same night, Rovers were back at the top of the division.

## Saturday 30 September 1989, Twerton Park

**Bristol Rovers** 0
**Reading** 0
**Half-time**: 0–0
**Attendance**: 6,120
**Referee**: Keith Cooper (Swindon)
**Bristol Rovers**: Martyn, Alexander, Twentyman, Yates, Mehew, Jones, Holloway, Reece, White, Penrice, Willmott. Substitutes: Cawley (not used), Sealy (not used).
**Reading**: Francis, Jones, Richardson, Beavon, Hicks, Wood, Knight, Gernon, Senior, Gilkes, Payne. Substitutes: Leworthy for Payne (63 mins), Bashir (not used).

During the week, Gerry Francis tried to sign an experienced goalkeeper on loan, as he was worried that playing Nigel Martyn, his England Under-21 player, would aggravate his knee injury. Rovers had two Western League goalkeepers – Glyn Thomas (Clevedon) and Mark Stevens (Mangotsfield) – registered on non-contract terms and a sixteen-year-old youth trainee. However, a specialist's diagnosis of a tendon strain below the left knee meant the problem could be treated sufficiently for Martyn to be included in an unchanged Rovers' starting line-up. Mid-table Reading included in their side prolific goalscorer Trevor Senior, who notched 5 goals in five days, defeating Newcastle United in the Littlewoods Cup and smashing a hat-trick against Swansea, and former Chelsea goalkeeper Steve Francis, whose previous encounter with Rovers ended in a hospital visit with a broken arm.

The goal needed to draw well-organised Reading out of their defensive shell failed to materialise, mainly due to Nigel Martyn's opposite number, Steve Francis, as Rovers' entertaining and powerful football in midfield failed to make the most of their advantage. Francis did particularly well to clear an Ian Holloway centre from David Mehew's feet early on, before twice making agile saves from Devon White. Rovers' striker then turned smartly to draw away from Wood but right-back Linden Jones, chasing back, brought him down and was booked for a professional foul.

On 18 minutes, Penrice shot wide following a free-kick and 2 minutes later Holloway fed the ball out to Mehew on the right, and as the cross came over, Penrice left the ball for White, whose shot was blocked. Rovers continued to create chances; Holloway chipped a shot just over the bar on the half hour, and 2 minutes before the break White squandered another good chance, after Twentyman's header had put him through, but goalkeeper Francis pushed his shot wide to the left for a corner.

Andy Reece has a strike on the Reading goal in the 0–0 home draw.

Following the break, White had an opportunity following an Ian Willmott corner, but was again thwarted by the Royals' defence, dominated by the two well-built and experienced central defenders Martin Hicks and Darren Wood. On the hour, Francis went full-length to deny Vaughan Jones a goal after good work by Andy Reece. Three minutes later, Reading sent on David Leworthy, a £105,000 buy from Spurs, as a substitute for Lee Payne and Rovers' tight grip on the game began to be loosened. Even so, there was only one occasion before Martyn's memorable late save that their goal was under serious threat. Martyn was backing onto the far post under pressure from Michael Gilkes when Linden Jones crossed the ball from Reading's right. The England Under-21 cap again illustrated his class by turning the centre behind for a corner. Geoff Twentyman blotted out Trevor Senior, and Steve Yates did an equally accomplished job on the speedy Michael Gilkes, but in the dying seconds of the game Reading came close to plundering a last-minute winner. Stuart Beavon broke fast down the right and sent over a teasing cross that was volleyed goalwards from close range by an unmarked Keith Knight. The powerful effort looked all over a winner until Nigel Martyn sprang to his left, acrobatically turning the ball round the post for a corner.

Rovers' manager nursed a secret in the dugout throughout the match, as his side failed to break down Reading's overworked defence. Wanting to bring off Ian Willmott who was starting to suffer with cramp, Francis had no one to send on, as his only other forward, Tony Sealy, had pulled a hamstring in the pre-match warm-up. Yearning for Sealy's pace which may have swung the game Rovers' way, the manager reflected, 'The longer it went on the more I worried Reading would snatch a last minute winner'. The result robbed Rovers of their 100 per cent home record, while maintaining Reading's undefeated away sequence and the two dropped points dashed Rovers' hopes of reclaiming the Third Division leadership.

## Saturday 7 October 1989, Twerton Park

**Bristol Rovers** 2 – Mehew, Penrice
**Fulham** 0
**Half-time**: 0–0
**Attendance**: 5,811
**Referee**: John Carter (Christchurch)
**Bristol Rovers**: Martyn, Jones, Twentyman, Yates, Mehew, Nixon, Holloway, Reece, White, Penrice, Willmott. Substitutes: Hazel for Nixon (87 mins), Cawley (not used).
**Fulham**: Stannard, Mauge, Thomas, Skinner, Nebbeling, Eckhardt, Marshall, Scott, Dowie, Sayer, Walker. Substitutes: Bremner for Skinner (74 mins), Watson (not used).

Rovers had fielded an unchanged team for the opening 8 league matches of the season, beating the previous record of 6 matches from the start of the 1947/48 and 1956/57 seasons. The sequence ended against Fulham through Ian Alexander's one match suspension, requiring Gerry Francis to reshuffle the defence, switching Vaughan Jones to the right side of the back-four, with Ian Willmott dropping back from the left-wing. Francis considered it too early to introduce summer signing Peter Cawley to a well-drilled defence and gave Paul Nixon, who had been waiting ten months for his chance, his full debut as an outside-left – a position he had never filled before – as Tony Sealy failed to respond to treatment on his hamstring injury. Fulham, tipped by many to be equipped to return to the Second Division, were only 2 points and two places behind Rovers, being unbeaten in their previous six outings after a shock home defeat by Tranmere Rovers on the opening day of the season. Queens Park Rangers' manager Trevor Francis was in the stand to check on Gary Penrice, who had already rejected a £500,000 move to Wimbledon, and goalkeeper Nigel Martyn, who was valued by Rovers' board at £1 million.

It was Penrice who set up the first chance after 2 minutes when he won the ball on the right touchline and centred to Mehew but the goalkeeper, Jim Stannard, saved well at the near post. It was the same combination which nearly broke the deadlock a few minutes later but Mehew's shot went a foot wide, following an Ian Willmott cross. And another typically crafty Penrice touch gave Mehew a third chance, but Stannard blocked the 8-yard angled shot with his knees for a corner. With 8 minutes gone, Rovers were fortunate to escape when Iain Dowie, on loan from Luton, won an aerial battle to knock the ball down to Andy Sayer and drove the return pass against the underside of Rovers' crossbar with a cracking 18-yard shot. Ian Holloway, playing his 200th game for Rovers, chipped the ball a foot over and Stannard did well to hold on to a near-post flick by Vaughan Jones. Andy Reece drove a free-kick over the bar after the goalkeeper had been penalised for 'steps', but Sayer's acrobatic scissors kick was only a foot away from giving Fulham the lead. Penrice missed the best opening of the first half when he hesitated for a fraction too long as the ball came through into the penalty area on the high wind, giving defender Jeff Eckhardt time to get a leg in and deflect wide for a corner.

Rovers took advantage of a John Marshall error after a poor Nebbeling backpass to take the lead in the 50th minute. The full-back's header was intended for his goalkeeper but Paul Nixon, making his full debut, intercepted and showed intelligence when he ignored an opportunity to shoot himself and instead pulled the ball back for the better-placed, and unmarked, David Mehew to drive into the empty net.

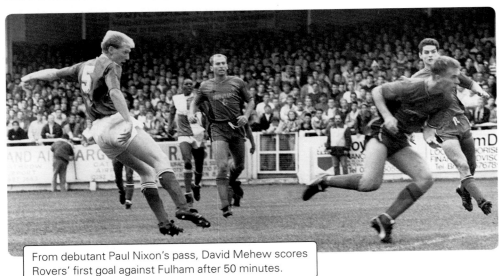

From debutant Paul Nixon's pass, David Mehew scores Rovers' first goal against Fulham after 50 minutes.

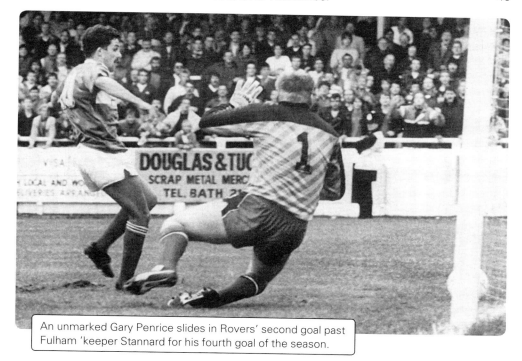

An unmarked Gary Penrice slides in Rovers' second goal past Fulham 'keeper Stannard for his fourth goal of the season.

Two minutes later, Devon White outjumped his marker Gavin Nebbeling to glance the ball to Mehew sprinting down the right beyond the Fulham defence. As he cut into the box, Mehew resisted the temptation to shoot and played the ball instead to an unmarked Penrice on the edge of the six-yard box, and he showed his finishing ability slotting the ball past the goalkeeper.

After the Rovers defender Geoff Twentyman fouled Peter Scott, both players tussled on the ground and were subsequently booked. Fulham's luck was out when Ronnie Mauge, a future Rovers player, headed in the resultant free-kick, only to have the goal ruled out for offside, although it appeared that a Rovers defender was standing on the goal line alongside Martyn. Rovers' key defender Steve Yates stifled Fulham's final rally, and even the late introduction of the experienced Des Bremner to replace the ineffective Justin Skinner, another future Rovers signing, made little difference. Fulham produced a final shot of merit with 3 minutes remaining, when Peter Scott, on the turn, curled a shot round the defence and off the outside of Martyn's left-hand post.

Fulham suffered their first away defeat of the campaign to a Rovers side that were setting remarkable early-season standards in defensive efficiency. Rovers' keeper Martyn kept a clean sheet for the eighth time in league and cup in the season and remarkably, he had played over 500 minutes without conceding a goal since the one at Bolton.

## Saturday 14 October 1989, Gigg Lane, Bury

Bury 0
Bristol Rovers 0
Half-time: 0–0
Attendance: 3,969
Referee: Arthur Smith (Birmingham)
Bury: Kelly, Hill, Withe, Hoyland, Valentine, Knill, Lee, Robinson, Cunningham, Feeley, Greenwood. Substitutes: Clements for Greenwood (23 mins), McIlroy (not used).
Bristol Rovers: Martyn, Alexander, Twentyman, Nixon, Mehew, Jones, Holloway, Reece, White, Penrice, Willmott. Substitutes: Sealy for Nixon (67 mins), Cawley (not used).

Rovers, seeking their first win at Gigg Lane since 24 March 1956, recalled Ian Alexander at right-back after a 1-match suspension, but lost defender Steve Yates, who started a 3-match ban; while skipper Vaughan Jones was playing his third different back-four position in as many games. Manager Francis still had the worry over Nigel Martyn's knee tendon strain as the goalkeeper had not trained with the team all week, and had missed the midweek England Under-21 game in Poland. There was also some doubt about who was to be selected on the left-hand side, as Paul Nixon had an ankle injury and Tony Sealy had been under treatment for a hamstring injury. Bury not only had a new manager in Sam Ellis, formerly at Blackburn Rovers, but had signed five new players for the start of the season. The combination seemed to be working as the Shakers, 1 place and 2 points behind second-placed Rovers, had picked up twelve of their 18 points away from home, but were also unbeaten at Gigg Lane.

Rovers' opening play was as bright as their yellow shirts, with the dangerous David Mehew causing problems down the right flank. The blond raider had a glorious chance to open the scoring after just 4 minutes when Penrice carved open the home defence, but Chris Withe managed to rob him with a last-ditch tackle. The Bury full-back was again on hand after 17 minutes to thwart Mehew a second time, after a Paul Nixon through ball sent him clear. Rovers survived a scare 10 minutes later when they failed to clear a corner and centre half Alan Knill shot narrowly wide from 4 yards. Andy Reece hit back immediately with a powerful shot into goalkeeper Kelly's body, and 2 minutes later Devon White climbed high above a melee of players, but directed his header from a Holloway corner over the bar. Nigel Martyn could only stand and watch as first David Lee struck the crossbar with a floated shot from the wing on 31 minutes, and then Andy Feeley clipped the woodwork with a snap shot 8 minutes later. Live-wire winger Lee inspired a string of dangerous attacks down the right and Ian Willmott had his work cut out trying to contain him. Rovers' efforts to put an end to his raids led to both Holloway and Reece having their names added to the referee's book.

As the home side took control in the second half, Rovers concentrated on protecting their injured 'keeper, who was playing his third game while unfit, and after the break they found themselves under siege for 25 minutes, relying on the counter-attack. Despite carrying an injury, Martyn capped a fine performance with a fingertip save from a looping Liam Robinson header following another centre from Lee after 53 minutes, and was the toast of the vociferous travelling fans 4 minutes later with a point-blank save from Cunningham's header as the Shakers turned up the pressure. He was called into action repeatedly in a full-blooded top-of-the-table clash despite a fine performance from Rovers' rearguard, well marshalled by captain Vaughan Jones and Geoff Twentyman. Penrice almost snatched all the points for Rovers with 11 minutes remaining when he escaped the close attentions of Knill and struck a fierce shot on the turn to bring out the best from Kelly. The goalkeeper did well to get behind the shot but could not hold the ball and dived along his line to gather it at the second attempt. Rovers' well-practised rearguard tactics managed to prevent Bury from scoring in a match for the first time all season. Also, with the Twerton Park men fighting hard for their sixth consecutive clean sheet, Nigel Martyn equalled Jim Eadie's club record for the third time since taking over the No. 1 jersey in 1987.

## Tuesday 17 October 1989, Ninian Park, Cardiff

**Cardiff City** 1 – Kelly
**Bristol Rovers** 1 – Mehew
**Half-time**: 0–0
**Attendance**: 6,372
**Referee**: John Moules (Erith)
**Cardiff City**: Hansbury, Rodgerson, Daniel, Barnard, Abraham, Perry, Lynex, Griffith, Kevan, Kelly, Pike. Substitute: Morgan for Pike (45 mins), Lewis (not used).
**Bristol Rovers**: Martyn, Alexander, Twentyman, Nixon, Mehew, Jones, Holloway, Reece, White, Penrice, Willmott. Substitutes: Sealy for Nixon (64 mins), Cawley (not used).

Andy Reece hits a left-foot shot that went just wide of the Cardiff City post.

Nigel Martyn approached the Severnside derby bidding to better his own club record of six consecutive clean sheets, and Jim Eadie's 6-match record set in Rovers' 1973/74 promotion season. Martyn had not let a goal in for 565 minutes; the last goal conceded was in the 1–0 defeat at Bolton Wanderers on the 9 September. Cardiff had made a poor start to the season but when Len Ashurst returned in September for a second spell as manager, following the departure of Frank Burrows, the City players had 'begun to play with more desire and passion', the new boss enthused.

Rovers opened brightly on a firm pitch but found Cardiff more spirited opponents than their league position suggested. Andy Reece was a couple of yards wide with an early shot; then in the 12th minute Devon White headed Ian Alexander's long ball towards David Mehew but he hooked it over the top. Martyn had to be alert after 20 minutes to deny Cohen Griffith, following a rare mistake by Vaughan Jones. Griffith intercepted a slack backpass and the quick Cardiff striker was clean through, but the Rovers goalkeeper stood up to him and the shot rebounded off his legs. Rovers' defence was still in disarray as Griffith picked up the rebound and found Chris Pike on the edge of the six-yard area, but his side-footed shot shaved the crossbar. The Bluebirds had much the better of the first-half exchanges, but White and Penrice combined again to send Mehew away down the right, after Penrice played a glorious cross-field ball, but the final cross was too near to 'keeper Roger Hansbury.

In the 47th minute, Paul Nixon was fouled in the penalty area by Ian Rodgerson and a penalty was awarded. Ian Holloway had the responsibility but he placed the low spot-kick to Roger Hansbury's right and the goalkeeper got his hands to the too-soft shot and pushed it out. Rovers then had a Penrice goal ruled out in the 59th minute when a linesman flagged as Devon White went for a back header, which came off the crossbar before Penrice headed in he rebound. Referee John Moules initially awarded the goal until he spotted his linesman. Hansbury made a quality save, hurling himself to keep out a perfect Penrice header, set up by Holloway's searching cross, turning the effort away for a corner. Rovers took the lead in the 71st minute with another of their well-executed corner routines. Penrice's header from a Holloway cross was brilliantly saved by Hansbury, resulting in another corner. Then Holloway's in-swinging corner came back in from the right, White met it but his header was blocked. Luckily the ball fell to Mehew by the far post, who pounced to crash in the loose ball.

Cardiff's equaliser came in the 80th minute from Mark Kelly, following a free-kick which was cleared to him 40 yards out near the touchline. The skilful midfielder advanced and responded to his manager's call to shoot more often by hitting a speculative left-foot drive from the edge of the penalty area, which Martyn seemed to have covered. Aimed for the far post, the drive from the right appeared to bobble in front of Rovers' goalkeeper and accelerated off the dewy turf over the goalkeeper's right arm before nestling in the back of the net. There were uncharacteristic signs of panic in Rovers' in the final 10 minutes, as the Bluebirds roused themselves following their equaliser. Ian Holloway had to clear a glancing Gareth Abraham header off his own goal line during Cardiff's final surge. Sixty seconds from time, Steve Lynex wasted a match winning chance by lifting his drive over the bar from Rodgerson's thoughtful cross.

The Rovers fans, who represented almost half of the crowd, were as relieved as the players and manager to return with a point, as Cardiff's late goal deprived Rovers of the Third Division leadership. It was the first goal to pass Nigel Martyn in 645 minutes, and the Rovers custodian, who otherwise played with customary assurance, needed to have kept his goal intact for another 63 minutes to beat Jim Eadie's record. However, the Cornishman easily beat his previous best marks of 555 and 580 minutes, when he twice completed 6 consecutive unbeaten games two seasons before. Gerry Francis refused to share the other players' sympathetic view that Martyn was unlucky in failing to prevent the equalising goal, 'My grandmother could have saved it – you don't expect an England Under-21 goalkeeper to let in goals like that,' he bitingly commented.

From an Ian Holloway corner, David Mehew reacts quickly to score Rovers' second goal at Ninian Park.

## 18 OCTOBER 1989

|                     | P  | W | D | L | F  | A  | Pts |
|---------------------|----|---|---|---|----|----|-----|
| Tranmere Rovers     | 11 | 7 | 1 | 3 | 25 | 8  | 22  |
| Bury                | 11 | 6 | 4 | 1 | 20 | 12 | 22  |
| BRISTOL ROVERS      | 11 | 6 | 4 | 1 | 12 | 4  | 22  |
| Rotherham United    | 11 | 6 | 3 | 2 | 26 | 12 | 21  |
| Bristol City        | 11 | 6 | 2 | 3 | 14 | 13 | 20  |
| Bolton Wanderers    | 11 | 5 | 4 | 2 | 15 | 11 | 19  |
| Huddersfield Town   | 11 | 5 | 4 | 2 | 15 | 13 | 19  |

## Saturday 21 October 1989, Twerton Park

Bristol Rovers 4 – White, Nixon, Holloway (penalty), Quow (own goal)
Northampton Town 2 – Brown, Barnes
Half-time: 0–1
Attendance: 4,920
Referee: Mike James (Horsham)
**Bristol Rovers**: Martyn, Alexander, Twentyman, Nixon, Mehew, Jones, Holloway, Reece, White, Penrice, Willmott. Substitutes: Sealy for Penrice (half-time), Cawley (not used).
**Northampton Town**: Gleasure, Quow, Gernon, Thomas, Wilcox, McPherson, Berry, Donald, Collins, Barnes, Brown. Substitutes: Sandeman for Brown (61 mins), Wilson (not used).

Rovers picked up two injuries at Ninian Park, but both Vaughan Jones (bruised and twisted right ankle) and Andy Reece (two stitches in his left thigh) were declared fit to face Northampton Town. Transfer interest in Gary Penrice had eased temporarily and the striker was hoping to add to his 3 league goals from 11 matches. Penrice believed the absence of winger Phil Purnell was a significant factor in his lack of goals. In fact, Rovers had scored just twelve times so far in the season, with only four other Third Division clubs netting fewer goals. Northampton had ended a sequence of three successive defeats with a 4–2 win over Blackpool on the Tuesday night. Bobby Barnes, the former West Ham United winger, signed from Bournemouth for £70,000, scored one of the goals for the improving mid-table side.

Rovers started badly on a wet pitch and were a goal down after only 4 minutes when Irvin Gernon's long range free-kick found Steve Brown alone in the box, the midfielder stooping to force his header past a stranded Nigel Martyn. Only the alertness of Rovers' goalkeeper, who advanced quickly to divert the shot with his boot, prevented Steve Berry from increasing Northampton's lead. Gradually, Rovers came back into the game and Devon White had a header cleared off the line, then hit the underside of the bar with a crashing header from a deep Ian Willmott cross, and had a fierce drive blocked. White turned provider when he outjumped the defence to direct his header for Holloway to volley right-footed, but Gleasure saved. Gary Penrice failed to come out for the second half as he was suffering great pain from a shoulder injury sustained in the first half. Rovers' physiotherapist, Roy Dolling, believed that Penrice had briefly dislocated his shoulder in the challenge, and so he was replaced by Tony Sealy. Rovers came close to equalising when, from an Alexander cross from the right, Devon White headed on to Geoff Twentyman at the far post, but the defender's rising shot hit the crossbar. It took the best part of an hour for Rovers to recover; Alexander set up the equaliser after 55 minutes with a centre from the right, which White tucked away for his first goal in 7 games, his outstretched leg squeezing in a shot at the near post.

Then Rovers appeared to have thrown the game away as Alexander contributed to Northampton regaining the lead 2 minutes later. He punched a right-side centre from Bobby Barnes over his own crossbar and Barnes easily scored the subsequent penalty, Martyn diving

Devon White falls to the ground but manages to score Rovers' first equalising goal, despite the attention of Northampton defender Keith McPherson.

Ian Holloway takes careful aim to score Rovers' third goal against Northampton from the penalty spot.

to his left while the ball went into the opposite corner. There were 11 minutes remaining when Devon White, who had plagued the Northampton defence all afternoon, again dashed into the penalty area. He failed to get in a shot but the ball broke to Paul Nixon, and the twenty-six-year-old volleyed in his first league goal from 15 yards. It was a crucial equaliser providing the springboard for an improbable victory, helped by the crowd's rousing enthusiasm.

Rovers remained on top, and 3 minutes from time, the irrepressible White bore down on the Cobblers' goal again. The desperate goalkeeper, Gleasure, could only grasp the striker's ankles as he attempted to go round him and conceded a clear penalty. Ian Holloway, who missed from the spot at Cardiff in midweek, was again entrusted with the kick, but this time he made no mistake, driving the ball low to the goalkeeper's left. It was his first goal of the season. Rovers completed the scoring in the final minute when Ian Alexander drove a low cross from the right, and as White challenged, Trevor Quow turned the ball into his own net.

Rovers finished the game at their scintillating best and stormed back to the top of the Third Division with a sensational comeback, but Gerry Francis was still not satisfied. The manager was happy with his team's magnificent fightback and aggressive attacking, but critical of the defensive play. 'Our whole defending – including the forwards and midfield – was sloppy and lethargic. There'll be a bit of work done on that this week,' he warned his table-topping squad.

## Saturday 28 October 1989, Sealand Road, Chester

Chester City 0
Bristol Rovers 0
**Half-time**: 0–0
**Attendance**: 2,618
**Referees**: Trelford Mills (Barnsley) and Mike Penn (Kingswinford)
**Chester City**: Stewart, Lightfoot, Hamilton, Abel, Reeves, Butler, Pugh, Woodthorpe, Hulme, Painter, Croft. Substitutes: Lundon for Reeves (75 mins), Wynne (not used)
**Bristol Rovers**: Martyn, Alexander, Twentyman, Yates, Mehew, Jones, Holloway, Reece, White, Sealy, Nixon. Substitutes: Cawley (not used), Willmott (not used).

Sealand Road was considered a 'happy hunting ground' for many of Rovers' players as it was there, eighteen months before, that Gerry Francis' cobbled-together side had started to become a force in the Third Division after beginning the season as the bookies' favourites for relegation. The 3–0 victory on 5 March was Rovers' first away win during the 1987/88 campaign, and triggered a remarkable run which swept them from 20th to a final position of 8th. Transfer-listed striker Gary Penrice, who had dislocated his left shoulder during the last match against Northampton, was ruled out of the game, resulting in him missing only his sixth game in more than three years. Defender Steve Yates returned to Rovers' back-four after a 3-match suspension, and Tony Sealy made his first start. Chester manager Harry McNally was desperately trying to sign a striker in time for the game after losing Carl Dale, the previous season's top scorer, with a badly-gashed knee and also England youth forward, Aiden Newhouse, with a hamstring injury. He rushed into the transfer-market and signed twenty-one-year-old Kevin Hulme on a month's loan from Bury.

Devon White was guilty of the miss of the match after 21 minutes of the first half, failing to hit the target from 4 yards when he smashed the ball high over the Chester bar following a

Ian Alexander wins an aerial duel with Chester's Brian Croft in the goalless draw at Sealand Road.

brilliant one-handed save by Billy Stewart from Nixon's point-blank header. The wasted chance was the highlight of a scrappy first half, not helped by the damp and blustery conditions. The only scoring opportunity the Rovers' defence allowed Chester was from a Brian Croft left-wing corner, 3 minutes before half-time. David Pugh was well placed as Rovers failed to clear properly, but he volleyed the ball high over Nigel Martyn's crossbar. Referee Trelford Mills retired at half-time with a pulled calf muscle sustained just before the interval and was replaced by substitute official Mike Penn.

The interval seemed to spark a resurgence in Chester's spirit and the lively winger Brian Croft, who had shown earlier promise, briefly burst into life giving full-back Ian Alexander a torrid time. Steve Yates made one excellent tackle early in the second half denying Rob Painter a good goal-scoring chance. Goalkeeper Stewart again did well to save, as Devon White was put clean through by Holloway's pinpoint pass and then 3 minutes later, Holloway crossed from Rovers' right to see another Nixon header go wide of the post. To add to Devon White's unhappy afternoon, the bustling striker was booked again in the 73rd minute, by the second referee of the match, and was duly sent off. His late tackle on Chester centre-back Chris Lightfoot added to an earlier booking for an off-the-ball incident with the same player, who had had his name taken for felling White in the 70th minute. Chester, weakened by injuries, belied their lowly league position and fought constantly without being able to find a way past the league's meanest defence, despite Rovers' obvious disadvantage, and they failed to trouble Nigel Martyn in the remaining quarter of the game.

Gerry Francis felt the game was spoilt by the blustery conditions, but a point kept Rovers on top of the Third Division and stretched their unbeaten run to an impressive 9 matches, much to the delight of Rovers' large travelling support, which had helped to swell Sealand Road to its biggest attendance of the season – 2,618.

### Wednesday 1 November 1989, Twerton Park

**Bristol Rovers** 2 – Nixon, Mehew
**Huddersfield Town** 2 – Cecere, Maskell
**Half-time**: 1–0
**Attendance**: 6,467
**Referee**: Alan Simmons (Cheadle Hulme)
**Bristol Rovers**: Martyn, Alexander, Twentyman, Yates, Mehew, Jones, Holloway, Reece, White, Sealy, Nixon. Substitutes: Cawley (not used), Willmott (not used).
**Huddersfield Town**: Hardwick, Marsden, Hutchings, May, O'Doherty, Lewis, Bent, Wilson, Cecere, Maskell, Smith. Substitutes: Withe for Smith (77 mins), O'Regan (not used).

Victory over Huddersfield Town would put Rovers 2 points clear at the top of the Third Division. With a third of the season gone, there was an increasing likelihood of a promotion duel developing with Bristol City, who were at last beginning to live up to their early rating as one of the division's top sides. However, Rovers' management team were anxious to hold off a suspension crisis as there were three players approaching the danger zone for bans under the penalty point system. Devon White was already certain of a ban after his sending off at Chester, and further bookings for Ian Holloway or Vaughan Jones could have caused bans to be imposed on them for passing 21 disciplinary points. 'It is a concern,' admitted assistant manager Kenny Hibbitt, 'but we have to try and curb the bookings without losing our competitiveness.' Huddersfield had lost only twice in the league – at Tranmere and at home to Cardiff – and like Rovers, they had kept a settled side. Former Nottingham Forest and England striker Peter Withe, Town's assistant manager, was added to the Terrier's squad.

Huddersfield took the game to Rovers from the kick-off, forcing a corner after just 8 seconds, but Paul Nixon's second league goal after 2 minutes gave Rovers a perfect start to the match. David Mehew exposed Huddersfield's shaky back-four with an

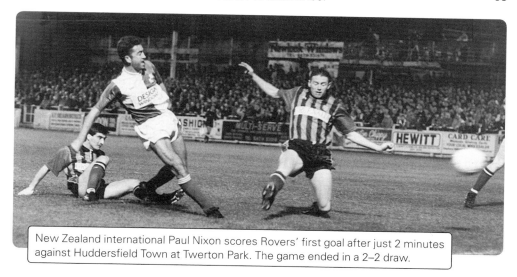

New Zealand international Paul Nixon scores Rovers' first goal after just 2 minutes against Huddersfield Town at Twerton Park. The game ended in a 2–2 draw.

incisive right-wing run and the New Zealand international moved through in the inside-right channel, avoiding a challenge from Robert Wilson, to steer the ball wide of goalkeeper Steve Hardwick, whose first touch was to pick it out of the net.

During the remainder of the first half, the Yorkshire side produced the best attacking football seen from a visiting team at Twerton during the season so far, and it took two good saves by Nigel Martyn to prevent the menacing Craig Maskell equalising. Martyn needed to be even more agile after the restart, as he turned a Wilson drive round the post for a corner. On the hour, Town's Robert Wilson and Rovers' Andy Reece were lectured at length by referee Alan Simmons, following a skirmish. Soon after, Tony Sealy, playing his first full home game for the Pirates, became involved in a fracas started by a clash between Wilson and Devon White. A mass brawl developed on the edge of the Huddersfield penalty area and Sealy was shown the red card, on 62 minutes, for felling Town's Welsh international defender, Dudley Lewis, with a punch. Maskell's late challenge on Martyn brought more stern words from the referee, but focus was returned to the footballing side of the contest when the Terriers equalised in the 69th minute. Sealy's dismissal clearly unsettled Rovers, and Huddersfield took full advantage. A shot from former Chelsea defender Chris Hutchings, after a 30-yard run, was

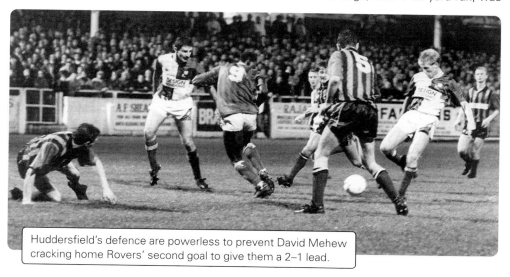

Huddersfield's defence are powerless to prevent David Mehew cracking home Rovers' second goal to give them a 2–1 lead.

parried by Martyn, and an alert Mike Cecere slotted home the loose ball from an acute angle. Yet Rovers depleted forces regained the lead in the 81st minute when Mehew thundered a fierce shot past Hardwick from the edge of the box, as Huddersfield's defence failed to clear an Ian Alexander free-kick.

It appeared that the visitors would undeservedly go home empty-handed, but a Vaughan Jones foul on tricky winger Junior Bent brought a last-gasp equaliser for his hometown club. The impressive Chris Marsden took the resulting free-kick from the right and Craig Maskell levelled the score with a near-post header. It was the fifth time during the season that Huddersfield had scored in the last minute to gain either a win or a draw.

Sealy became the fourth Rovers player to be dismissed since the start of the season and further highlighted the club's disappointing disciplinary record. Most importantly, Rovers failed to gain the victory needed to open a 2-point gap on their promotion rivals on a night of high drama in front of Twerton Park's biggest crowd of the season.

## Saturday 4 November 1989, Twerton Park

**Bristol Rovers** 1 – Sealy
**Blackpool** 1 – Madden
**Half-time**: 0–0
**Attendance**: 5,520
**Referee**: Dennis Hedges (Oxford)
**Bristol Rovers**: Martyn, Alexander, Twentyman, Yates, Mehew, Jones, Holloway, Reece, White, Sealy, Nixon. Substitutes: Willmott for Holloway (half-time), Cawley (not used).
**Blackpool**: Bartram, Burgess, Morgan, Coughlin, Methven, Elliott, Owen, Madden, Hawkins, Garner, Briggs. Substitutes: Sinclair for Hawkins (88 mins), Wright (not used).

In an interview published in the *Western Daily Press* on the morning of the match, Gerry Francis admitted that he was disappointed that the achievements of table-topping Rovers were being clouded by their poor disciplinary record, but he did feel that the four dismissals made their position as Third Division leaders all the more creditable. In fact, Rovers had not lost any of the games in which a player had been sent off, but having played 130 minutes of football out of the 14 league games with ten players, Francis was 'a little fed up of playing with ten men'. Striker Gary Penrice was still out with his shoulder injury, and Nigel Martyn was set to make his 100th appearance for Bristol Rovers. Blackpool, hovering above the relegation zone, included former Bristol City players Gordon Owen and Nigel Hawkins in their squad.

Rovers were neat and inventive from the outset, but were disrupted early on when playmaker Ian Holloway was hit in the face by the ball as he mistimed a header. However, he carried on playing while clutching a sponge to his head as he tried to clear his vision. Twice referee Dennis Hedges asked whether he wanted to carry on with his injured eye

Experienced Blackpool defender Colin Methven wins the battle for the ball with David Mehew.

– which he did – but the mishap was directly responsible for a bad miss which cost Rovers the chance to go into an early lead, which their skill – if not their commitment – deserved. Paul Nixon began a move deep in his own half with a touchline run that carried him past two challenges, before delivering a deep cross for Tony Sealy to provide the final pass into Holloway. There was a clear chance but with his blurred vision he smashed the ball well wide of the target. Holloway did not appear after the interval and was replaced by Ian Willmott.

Martyn was a virtual spectator until 3 minutes from half-time when he pushed away an Andy Garner header, and as the ball ran loose, Yates blocked Colin Methven's shot on Rovers' goal line. Rovers were finding it difficult to break down a solid Blackpool defence, controlled by the experienced centre half Methven. Devon White brought a smart save from Vince Bartram, and then the closest the home side came to scoring was a header from White that came back off the visitor's crossbar. Chances continued to be created through David Mehew, Rovers' most threatening player, and twice Bartram saved well, but Mehew's best chance was wasted as he failed to control a cleverly scooped lob by Jones. Nigel Hawkins tested Martyn in the 58th minute with a first-time shot from Steve Morgan's centre.

Rovers must have thought that the game would swing their way when Blackpool's right-back, Dave Burgess, was sent off in the 73rd minute by referee Dennis Hedges, afer he took a swipe at Steve Yates on the touchline, leaving the defender clutching his head. But 7 minutes after the dismissal, the Tangerines took the lead when Craig Madden deflected a long-range shot from Russell Coughlin past Nigel Martyn, ending his hopes of a clean sheet on his 100th appearance for Rovers. Francis' men were facing their first home defeat for nine months, but kept pushing forward with time running out and with only 2 minutes remaining, Vaughan Jones struck an excellent cross-field pass to his full-back partner, Ian Alexander, on the right. The Scotsman's low cross, following a strong run, was side-footed in from close range by Tony Sealy, to score his first goal for the Pirates.

Although some way from their best, Rovers at least deserved the point and from the amount of possession they enjoyed should have won. A Rovers win would have seen them retain the leadership of the Third Division, but the two dropped points against Blackpool meant they finished the day in 2nd position, behind the team who now topped the division for the first time – Bristol City. The last time both City and Rovers stood together at the top of the table had been 16 September 1964.

Fallen defender Gary Briggs is unable to prevent Tony Sealy scoring Rovers' late equaliser against Blackpool – the striker's first goal for the club.

## Tuesday 7 November 1989, Plainmoor, Torquay
## Leyland Daf Cup Southern Preliminary Round Group 2

**Torquay United** 1 – Loram
**Bristol Rovers** 1 – White
**Half-time**: 0–0
**Attendance**: 2,218
**Referee**: Paul Durkin (Portland)
**Torquay United**: Veysey, Holmes, Lloyd, Elliott, Matthews, Joyce, Loram, Airey, Edwards, Uzzell, Weston. Substitutes: Smith (J) (not used), Taylor (not used).
**Bristol Rovers**: Martyn, Alexander, Twentyman, Yates, Mehew, Jones, Holloway, Reece, White, Sealy, Nixon. Substitutes: Cawley (not used), McClean (not used).

Torquay United had knocked Rovers out of the Leyland Daf competition twice in past years, and the previous season they had enjoyed a trip to Wembley before losing 4–1 to Bolton Wanderers in the final. Since manager Dave Smith's appointment in October, Fourth Division Torquay had won 3 matches, drawn 2 and lost only 1, and included former Rovers midfield player Ian Weston, but Paul Smith, also signed from Rovers, was absent with a knee ligament injury. Thankfully, the eye injury Ian Holloway suffered against Blackpool did not rule him out for selection, despite the fact he temporarily lost sight in his left eye and underwent a scan on his skull, and so he was available for the Leyland Daf Cup match. As the Rovers squad prepared for the match, the *Bristol Evening Post* reported that the Rovers board were considering bids totalling close to £1.5 million for Nigel Martyn and Gary Penrice. First Division Crystal Palace were prepared to match Rovers' £1 million valuation of goalkeeper Martyn, named the previous day for the England B squad. While Second Division Watford had made an offer approaching £500,000 for striker Penrice, who had been out of the team for 3 matches with a shoulder injury, but who had resumed training on the previous Monday, despite it being unlikely that he would play at Torquay.

Rovers struggled to get to grips with Torquay's early energetic approach, with Nigel Martyn saving well from Mark Loram and Dean Edwards, but the visitors should have taken the lead in the 34th minute. Paul Nixon carved a gaping hole in the United defence, but Devon White's tame shot was smothered by goalkeeper Ken Veysey. Nigel Martyn, the cornerstone of a Rovers defence besieged by a talented Torquay side at the beginning of both halves was back into the thick of the action as the Devon side mounted another assault, but was helpless to stop Torquay snatching the lead in the 61st minute. Airey, from a cross, nodded the ball to Loram whose original strike was kicked off the line by Ian Alexander, but the striker followed up to plant the ball in the back of the net. It was only a temporary set-back as within 3 minutes Rovers were level. Andy Reece's corner was floated over, and the 6ft 4in White was allowed to outjump Veysey to flick the ball into the goal; it was his first away goal for two seasons. Rovers played their best football following the equaliser and began to stamp their Third Division authority on the game with Tony Sealy and Paul Nixon creating problems for the Torquay defence. They were desperately unlucky not to grab the winner with 11 minutes remaining when, after rounding two defenders Nixon's 'goal' was disallowed as Mehew was ruled offside. And with 2 minutes remaining, Mehew went close to scoring a winner from Nixon's left wing centre. However, Rovers got their Leyland Daf Cup campaign off to a satisfactory start at Plainmoor, and extended their unbeaten run to 12 games.

## Saturday 11 November 1989, Gay Meadow, Shrewsbury

**Shrewsbury Town** 2 – McGinlay, Griffiths
**Bristol Rovers** 3 – Sealy 2, Holloway
**Half-time**: 1–1
**Attendance**: 4,746
**Referee**: Trevor Simpson (Halifax)
**Shrewsbury Town**: Perks, Green, Pittman, Kelly, Finley, Moyes, Brown, Hartford, Worsley, McGinlay, Naughton. Substitutes: Griffiths for Brown (27 mins), Priest for Naughton (63 mins).
**Bristol Rovers**: Martyn, Alexander, Twentyman, Yates, Mehew, Jones, Holloway, Reece, McClean, Sealy, Nixon. Substitutes: Cawley (not used), Willmott (not used).

Shrewsbury started the match in 8th place in the table with 25 points, three less than Rovers, having won 5 of their 7 home fixtures. The home side were without suspended midfield player Jon Purdie, but included thirty-nine-year-old player-coach Asa Hartford, the former Scotland international, and the ex-Bristol City defender David Moyes. Rovers, although defeated just once on their travels, had scored three and conceded only 2 goals away from home in 7 league games. Christian McClean was given his first full appearance of the season in place of the suspended Devon White.

   After only 11 minutes, there was a real let-off for the Shrews when Holloway set up Mehew from 6 yards, but Rovers' leading scorer shot into Perks diving body. In the 16th minute, Mick Brown had the Rovers defence in trouble. Leaving two defenders stranded, he crossed for former Yeovil Town striker John McGinlay, who slipped away from his marker, Steve Yates, to

Nigel Martyn, pictured with mascot Dean Matthews, before his last game for the club at Shrewsbury Town.

Ian Holloway takes aim to score Rovers' second goal after 65 minutes in the 3–2 win at Gay Meadow.

glance home a header just inside the far post for the opening goal. But in the 27th minute, with Brown off the field with suspected concussion, Christian McClean centred for Tony Sealy to score the equaliser. David Mehew brought the ball out of midfield for McClean to deliver a dipping centre, and with goalkeeper Perks rooted to the spot, Sealy raced in unmarked to side-foot the ball home from 5 yards out. Once level, Rovers took command, but good saves by Perks from Sealy, Holloway and a thunderous 25-yard drive from Reece kept the scores level until the interval. There was plenty of cut and thrust from the two teams chasing the top spot and there was nothing in it at 1–1 just into the second half. Shrewsbury were beginning to get on top through the skills of Willie Naughton, until he was sent sprawling by Ian Alexander, but the Rovers full-back, booked only minutes earlier after a clash with Asa Hartford, went unpunished by referee Trevor Simpson. Naughton was carried off in the 65th minute and before substitute Phil Priest could take over Ian Holloway powered the ball into the net from 20 yards, after good work from Paul Nixon.

Shrewsbury, with some justification, felt aggrieved, as it was the second time Rovers had scored when they were down to ten men. Four minutes after Holloway's effort, Rovers were pegged back when their disorganised defence was pierced by Griffiths' close-range downward header following a dropped ball by Martyn, after Twentyman scooped it off the line from McGinlay's initial header. But inside 4 minutes, after clever work on the left by Nixon, it was Sealy's deadly finishing which gave Rovers a hard-earned victory. His winner was a classic strike, turning defender Steve Pittman and then thumping a shot from the edge of the penalty area low to Perks' left. With only seconds remaining, there was more drama to come. Nigel Martyn became stranded and was beaten by Town substitute Carl Griffiths, an equaliser looked to be on the way until the dependable Twentyman cleared off the line.

Rovers' outstanding player Tony Sealy scored 2 goals and set up the third. He was beginning to benefit from match practice and a growing awareness of his new team's patterns of play.

However, he had even more cause now to regret the moment of madness that led to him being sent off, particularly so with the planned departure of Gary Penrice to Watford; the striker was starting a 3-match ban after the punch-throwing incident in the match against Huddersfield Town. In what was likely to have been his last game for Rovers, Nigel Martyn was beaten twice, which doubled his tally of goals conceded in the 7 previous away league games that season.

With Bristol City's failure to win at home, Rovers regained the Third Division leadership and stretched their unbeaten run to 13 matches, to the delight of more than 1,000 Rovers fans at Gay Meadow. It was Rovers' 13th game without defeat and they might well have reflected on it as lucky 13 in many ways.

## Saturday 18 November 1989, Twerton Park. FA Cup First Round

**Bristol Rovers** 1 – Reece
**Reading** 1 – Conroy
**Half-time**: 1–1
**Attendance**: 6,115
**Referee**: Danny Vickers (Ilford)
**Bristol Rovers**: Parkin, Alexander, Twentyman, Yates, Mehew, Jones, Holloway, Reece, McClean, Willmott, Nixon. Substitutes: Hazel for Willmott (82 mins), Cawley (not used).
**Reading**: Francis, Jones, Gilkes, Beavon, Hicks, Wood, Knight, Tait, Senior, Conroy, Payne. Substitutes: Whittock for Gilkes (half-time), Moran (not used).

Rovers moved quickly to replace £1 million sale Nigel Martyn by signing Brian Parkin, aged twenty-four, from Crystal Palace on a three-month loan. Parkin was registered by Rovers on the previous Saturday night, shortly after playing in his club's First Division game with Luton Town at Selhurst Park. Speedy action was necessary because only players signed seven days

Christian McClean stretches for the ball during the FA Cup tie with Reading.

in advance were eligible for the FA Cup. The league rule that a loan goalkeeper could be signed within twenty-four hours of a game did not apply. Rovers were now down to a bare thirteen players as a result of the transfers of Martyn and Penrice, the suspensions of strikers Devon White and Tony Sealy, and the long-term injuries of Phil Purnell and Billy Clark. Reading were keen to impress their new manager Ian Porterfield, former assistant manager to Bobby Campbell at Chelsea, who had joined the Royals in October.

Trevor Senior ought to have done better with a couple of early opportunities but it was Vaughan Jones who spurred Parkin's greatest action. His 19th-minute backpass was too short and Parkin was forced to make a smothering save at the feet of the advancing Senior. Nixon could have put Rovers ahead after 20 minutes when he rose to head a Christian McClean cross, but a nudge from behind ruined the resulting header which lacked power, and defender Linden Jones was fortunate not to concede a penalty for the push; Steve Francis was able to make a comfortable save. McClean also went close with a header, before Reading took the lead after 35 minutes.

Lee Payne struck a shot from the left which was charged down by the Rovers defence and Mike Conroy shot home past Brian Parkin. McClean sent in some dangerous crosses and almost got an equaliser after 43 minutes, before Ian Holloway had a 25-yard shot tipped over the crossbar. The home side were back in the hunt on the stroke of half-time when Nixon shielded the ball from Reading's defenders, he waited for Andy Reece to race in and the midfielder powerfully drove the ball high into the net past Francis for his first goal of the season.

Rovers went close after 50 minutes when Ian Holloway sent in a corner, which was met by Vaughan Jones but his namesake, Linden Jones, booked moments before after heavily felling Steve Yates with a late tackle, cleared off Reading's goal line. Reading goalkeeper Francis made two excellent saves to frustrate Rovers' depleted attack. First, the former Chelsea keeper leapt to tip a long-range Holloway shot over the crossbar. Then, 15 minutes from the end, he flung himself to turn an Ian Willmott drive wide of the near post.

Brian Parkin made a sound debut behind Rovers' tight defence, and Christian McClean showed some excellent touches. While Paul Nixon showed that he could be one of the choices to take over the mantle of the departed Penrice. Gerry Francis' main concern was having enough players to play league games rather than the FA Cup competition, although he did concede that the Cup was a good way to earn money.

## Tuesday 21 November 1989, Elm Park, Reading. FA Cup First Round replay

**Reading** 1 – Senior
**Bristol Rovers** 1 – Mehew
**Half-time**: 0–0
**Attendance**: 6,015
**Referee**: Danny Vickers (Ilford)
**Reading**: Francis, Jones, Richardson, Beavon, Hicks, Wood, Knight, Tait, Senior, Conroy, Payne. Substitutes: Moran for Knight (90 mins), Whitlock for Wood (106 mins).
**Bristol Rovers**: Parkin, Alexander, Twentyman, Yates, Mehew, Jones, Holloway, Reece, McClean, Willmott, Nixon. Substitutes: Cawley (not used), Hazel (not used).

Gerry Francis had faced a few player crises during his three seasons at Bristol Rovers, but few were as limiting as the one that hung over him prior to the FA Cup replay at Reading. The manager was unsure of having thirteen fit players registered for the Cup. Captain Vaughan Jones played through a bout of flu in the first match but if he failed to fully recover, it would leave only twelve fit players, and a strong possibility that Francis would have to name himself as a substitute. Unfortunately, assistant manager Kenny Hibbitt was not registered for the FA Cup. However, Rovers' boss did find some compensation in the replay as it was one more game towards clearing the suspension of strikers White and Sealy.

Early in the match Brian Parkin pushed a Lee Payne rocket over the crossbar and from the resulting corner-kick was well placed to turn aside Stuart Beavon's header. Keith Knight headed wide from a few yards out when he should have tested Parkin, while Trevor Senior was guilty of a glaring miss when clean through on goal. Rovers' attacking moments in the first half were an embarrassment for a side sitting proudly on top of the Third Division. Reading goalkeeper Francis was not forced to make a direct save as Rovers' attacking duo, Paul Nixon and Christian McClean, who had only played 8 first-team games between them, lacked ideas against the defensive towers of Martin Hicks and Darren Wood.

There was little respite for Rovers' hard-pressed defence at the start of the second half with Payne and Beavon firing in shots on Parkin's goal. Rovers eventually mustered their first shot of the game in the 61st minute, Nixon pulling the ball back from the byline for Mehew to crash a shot into the body of Steve Francis. But the storm continued at the other end as Parkin made three more spectacular saves in quick succession to keep Reading's rampant attack at bay. Rovers almost snatched an unlikely winner 5 minutes from the end of normal time, but Mehew's shot was directed just wide of Francis' left-hand post, and the game moved into an extra 30 minutes. Four minutes into extra time David Mehew broke the deadlock with his seventh goal of the season. Vaughan Jones, who shrugged off a bout of flu to lead the side well, eased the ball onto his right foot by the left touchline and his cross was deftly back-headed into the opposite corner of the goal by Mehew. With 2 minutes of the replay remaining, the team with the best defensive record in the Football League finally buckled, as former Watford striker Trevor Senior took the tie into a third match. Mike Conroy's deep cross from the right was headed across goal by Mick Tait, the ball shot off Senior's thigh and rolled into the goal from 8 yards out.

The most satisfying job Francis undertook on the night was to the win the toss in the referee's dressing room for the choice of venues for the third match. The eventual winners would meet Gillingham or non-league Welling in the third round. One bonus for Rovers was the form of Brian Parkin, on a three-month loan from Crystal Palace, who looked a more than adequate replacement for Nigel Martyn, who watched the game from the stand.

## Saturday 25 November 1989, Twerton Park

**Bristol Rovers** 2 – Mehew, White
**Swansea City** 0
**Half-time**: 1–0
**Attendance**: 5,623
**Referee**: David Elleray (Harrow-on-the-Hill)
**Bristol Rovers**: Parkin, Alexander, Twentyman, Yates, Mehew, Jones, Holloway, Reece, White, Hazel, Nixon. Substitutes: McClean for Hazel (88 mins), Cawley (not used).
**Swansea City**: Freestone, Hough, Coleman, Melville, Boyle, Thornber, Harris, Curtis, Legg, Raynor, Hutchison. Substitutes: Hughes for Curtis (45 mins), Phillips for Legg (82 mins).

Rovers' physiotherapist Roy Dolling worked overtime on nineteen-year-old defender Steve Yates, treating two painful kicks he received in the FA Cup replay at Reading. With goalkeeper Brian Parkin making his league debut for Rovers and still settling into the side, manager Gerry Francis was keen to field the defence who had proved so mean this season. Yates' partnership with Geoff Twentyman had made a major contribution to a defensive record of just 15 goals conceded in 20 matches. Devon White returned from his three-match suspension in place of Christian McClean to form a new striking partnership with Paul Nixon. During the week, Swansea had signed three new players but found only one of them, John Hughes, a £70,000 buy from Berwick Rangers was match fit. The Swans, lying in 11th place in the table, also included forty-two-year-old Tommy Hutchison, English football's oldest professional at the time.

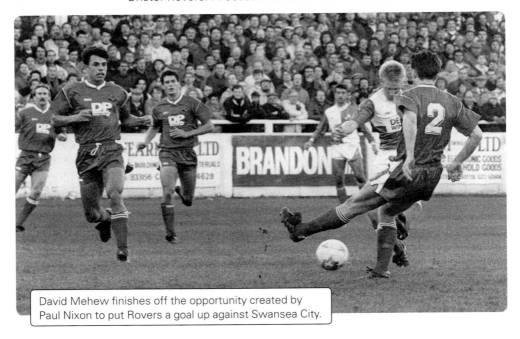

David Mehew finishes off the opportunity created by
Paul Nixon to put Rovers a goal up against Swansea City.

Swansea had nothing to offer apart from a massed defence and the ever inventive touches of Hutchison. Although Hutchison's skill had been good enough to win at Ashton Gate a few games previously, this time he only had Paul Raynor, the former Rovers loan signing, up front. The first of Nixon's telling crosses in the match saw White send a header skimming along the top of the Swansea crossbar and it was Nixon who unlocked the game with a delightful through ball into David Mehew's run in the 38th minute. Mehew struck his left-footed shot perfectly, but Roger Freestone threw himself down and got a hand to the ball, which took the

Devon White puts a simple header past Swansea goalkeeper
Roger Freestone to score Rovers' second goal at Twerton Park.

pace off it, but the ball squirmed away and rolled slowly across the line inside his left-hand post. It was perhaps a slightly lucky strike, but Rovers were well worth their lead after all their hard work.

New Swansea signing Hughes stayed on the bench until half-time when he took over from Welsh veteran Alan Curtis. Swansea wanted to give Raynor some support in his lonely vigil as their only attacker. They worked out a couple of good moves, aided by one run from Hutchison which carried him past three Rovers players to test the home defence. And Raynor had the ball whipped away for a corner as he was shaping up for a shot on goal. A rather bruising battle between White and Terry Boyle developed as White was nudged and pushed but continued challenging in the air and winning the ball successfully. Shortly after the hour mark, Nixon broke away down the right and received Holloway's cross-field pass, and looked up to see White heading for the far post. His deep cross was impeccably placed for the striker to stretch up and his downward header gave Freestone no chance. It was the former Boston United man's fifth goal of the season.

The Welsh club had come with the sole intention of frustrating Rovers' promotion charge, stringing five men across the middle of the park. It was the measure of Rovers' superiority that the visitors mustered just one shot all afternoon. With Ian Holloway and Andy Reece controlling the midfield, Rovers' back four, in particular Vaughan Jones, were able to 'stroll' through the game, never seriously in trouble. Gerry Francis described his team's win as 'competent' as Rovers stretched their unbeaten run to 16 games and kept them top of Division Three.

## 25 NOVEMBER 1989

|  | P | W | D | L | F | A | Pts |
|---|---|---|---|---|---|---|---|
| BRISTOL ROVERS | 17 | 9 | 7 | 1 | 24 | 11 | 34 |
| Rotherham United | 17 | 9 | 5 | 3 | 38 | 17 | 32 |
| Tranmere Rovers | 17 | 10 | 2 | 5 | 36 | 16 | 32 |
| Bristol City | 17 | 9 | 4 | 4 | 22 | 16 | 31 |
| Bury | 17 | 8 | 6 | 3 | 28 | 20 | 30 |
| Notts County | 17 | 8 | 6 | 3 | 24 | 17 | 30 |
| Bolton Wanderers | 17 | 7 | 7 | 3 | 22 | 15 | 28 |

## Monday 27 November 1989, Twerton Park. FA Cup First Round second replay

Bristol Rovers 0
Reading 1 – Senior
Half-time: 0–1
Attendance: 6,782
Referee: Keith Cooper (Pontypridd)
**Bristol Rovers:** Parkin, Alexander, Twentyman, Yates, Mehew, Jones, Holloway, Reece, White, Sealy, Nixon. Substitutes: McClean for Reece (81 mins), Hazel (not used).
**Reading:** Francis, Jones, Richardson, Beavon, Hicks, Whitlock, Knight, Tait, Senior, Conroy, Payne. Substitutes: Taylor for Payne (81 mins), Moran (not used).

Gerry Francis approached the third meeting with Reading caught somewhere between hope and anxiety. He hoped Rovers would come through with a victory – it was about time they had a run in one of the cup competitions – but the anxiety was there because of the risks of bookings or injuries which would devastate his small squad. Tony Sealy was restored to the Rovers attack following a three-match suspension, with the previous Saturday's hero Paul Nixon dropping back into midfield, while Ian Hazel was omitted. Rovers were looking to contain Reading danger man Trevor Senior, who had scored one of the eight hat-tricks of his career against the Pirates in a Milk Cup tie at Elm Park in 1986. Geoff Twentyman had made

Paul Nixon's shot beats Reading goalkeeper Steve Francis but goes wide of the post.

Tony Sealy gets in front of Reading defender Mark Whitlock to head for goal in the FA Cup replay defeat.

his Rovers debut that day as a central defender, but for four meetings since then Senior had not scored against him, until the previous week's replay of course. Extra time was to be played if the scores were level after 90 minutes, with a third replay at Elm Park on the following Thursday if necessary.

Devon White was first to test Reading goalkeeper Steve Francis in the 6th minute, then leading goalscorer David Mehew skied a good chance over the crossbar. As Rovers strove to end the stalemate tempers flared and Ian Alexander was cautioned for aiming a kick at Royal's veteran Mick Tait. Rovers stepped up the pace at the start of the second half and Andy Reece squandered his side's best chance in the 47th minute after Devon White had carved a gaping hole in the Reading back line. Reading's hard-pressed defence were again fortunate to escape in the 63rd minute when Sealy's snap header from a Mehew pass brushed the crossbar.

Reading were virtually anonymous as an attacking force, and until they squandered a penalty in the 70th minute they had not managed a goal attempt of any description. The penalty award completed an unhappy night for Ian Alexander, who had been booked in the first half. He failed to control the ball on the edge of the penalty area, turned and brought down Mick Conroy who was cutting in towards goal. The referee had no hesitation in pointing to the spot, but Rovers were reprieved when Brian Parkin dived to his left to stop Stuart Beavon's spot kick with his legs.

However, Rovers' relief was short-lived. Reading took the lead with a corner-kick routine introduced by new manager Ian Porterfield. The Royals stationed three big men on the edge of the penalty area and as Lee Payne's right wing corner came over, Trevor Senior checked and then made a darting run into the box to finish with an unstoppable header into the roof of the net. Francis' side were left to mount one last desperate effort to salvage a late equaliser, when Mehew, once again the inspiration in Rovers' midfield, burst through the resolute defence and shot with a clear sight on goal, but he was denied by another goal-line clearance from Linden Jones.

Gerry Francis' view was that the defeat would enhance his side's promotion bid as they had more chance of getting out of the Third Division than winning the FA Cup, commenting, 'With a small staff, too many cup-ties and replays stretch both our resources and players' powers of recovery from minor knocks.' Rovers' boss became a potential long-term target for Queens Park Rangers, seeking a manager after Trevor Francis' dismissal on that day. But the London club had to be prepared to wait until the end of the season, as Rovers made it clear that Francis would not be released from his contract, which was due to run out that following May.

## Saturday 2 December 1989, Fellows Park, Walsall

**Walsall** 1 – Bertschin
**Bristol Rovers** 2 – White, Mehew
**Half-time**: 1–1
**Attendance**: 4,038
**Referee**: David Phillips (Barnsley)
**Walsall**: Green, Wilder, Mower, Goodwin, Forbes, Skipper, Kelly, Rimmer, Bertschin, Marsh, Thorpe. Substitutes: Saville (not used), Gritt (not used).
**Bristol Rovers**: Parkin, Alexander, Twentyman, Willmott, Mehew, Jones, Holloway, Reece, White, Sealy, Nixon. Substitutes: Cawley for Willmott (28 mins), McClean (not used).

Steve Yates failed a fitness test on the morning of the match and was ruled out of the Rovers side because of a twisted knee, despite daily treatment following the FA Cup defeat on the previous Monday. Gerry Francis reverted to the formation used successfully when Yates was suspended, with Vaughan Jones playing alongside Geoff Twentyman in the centre of defence and Ian Willmott at left-back. Willmott came through a reserve match at Swansea on the previous Tuesday after dropping out of the senior squad because of ankle trouble. Midfielder Andy Reece returned to the club that rejected him as a youngster. Walsall, with a wretched record, had lost their last four home league and Cup games without scoring a goal. Indeed, they had scored only 15 goals all season and were sitting in 22nd place in the table. Against the Saddlers, Rovers came up against a former teammate, goalkeeper Ron Green, who played for Wimbledon, Manchester City and Shrewsbury Town after leaving Rovers for Scunthorpe United in 1986, and was now back with his original club.

Walsall began with a burst of pressure, Parkin having to pull down a high cross from Marsh, while another good move ended with the 'keeper punching away from the same player, as Wilder's follow up was blocked. Rovers were penned back for a while but suddenly broke out quickly, Nixon playing a neat ball for Andy Reece to chase but Forbes pulled off a smart sliding tackle. Walsall took the lead in the 13th minute when Mower burst through on the left and found Rimmer, whose pass saw Marsh turn inside to cross quickly with his right foot. Keith Bertschin was there unmarked to score with a powerful header into the roof of the net.

Devon White rises above the Walsall defence to head Rover's equalising goal from Andy Reece's corner.

A minute into the second half and David Mehew puts Rovers into the lead at Fellows Park, scoring past former Rovers 'keeper Ron Green.

Three minutes later Twentyman brought down Thorpe. He touched the resulting free-kick to Mower who then bent a left-foot shot over the wall, but Parkin made a magnificent save in the angle of the bar and post. Rovers produced a dangerous raid in the 29th minute when White cut in before finding Nixon, and Ron Green had to dive down at the winger's feet to save. A minute later, Pete Cawley was sent on for the limping Willmott and his first appearance of the season, taking up position in the back-four. Twice in a minute Rovers created good chances, but Green saved at the feet of White when Cawley headed on a free-kick, and again as Mehew made a second attempt. Walsall almost took a commanding lead in the 38th minute when a Bertschin header was held on the line by Brian Parkin. Three minutes from the break Rovers equalised after a mistake by Bertschin. His poor backpass led to the visitors forcing a corner and Devon White climbed highest at the far post to head in Reece's cross.

Rovers made a sensational start to the second half, going ahead only 20 seconds after the restart. Jones hoisted the ball down the middle, Sealy lobbed it into the goalmouth, two Walsall defenders failed to clear and Mehew rammed the ball low into the net for his eighth league goal of the season. Mower was booked in the 52nd minute for a blatant trip on Tony Sealy who was through on goal, but the Saddlers went close to equalising 10 minutes later. Rimmer showed determination to win the ball and find Marsh whose low left-foot drive raced just wide. Shortly after Sealy forced a fine save from Green. Fifteen minutes from the end Parkin made sure of victory with a splendid save from Stuart Rimmer, and in the 88th minute Rimmer shot wide with another chance to equalise. Late on Mehew failed to hit the target at the other end from 8 yards out. Walsall's Graham Forbes and Rovers' Tony Sealy were booked for an injury-time flare-up.

About 1,500 Rovers fans gave their team tremendous backing throughout the match and showed their delight as the players left the field. A chorus of 'Going up, Going up' rang out, as their favourites increased their unbeaten league run to 14 games and opened up a 4-point lead at the top of the table.

## Friday 15 December 1989, Gresty Road, Crewe

---

**Crewe Alexandra** 1 – Swain
**Bristol Rovers** 0
**Half-time**: 0–0
**Attendance**: 3,473
**Referee**: Alan Dawson (Jarrow)
**Crewe Alexandra**: Greygoose, Dyson, Callaghan, Smart, Swain, Murphy, Walters, Edwards, Joseph, Sussex, Fishenden. Substitutes: Easter for Joseph (80 mins), McKearney (not used).
**Bristol Rovers**: Parkin, Cawley, Twentyman, Yates, Mehew, Jones, Holloway, Reece, White, Sealy, Nixon. Substitutes: Hazel for Nixon (68 mins), McClean (not used).

Rovers agreed to Crewe's request to bring forward the Third Division match from Saturday 16 December to the Friday night. Victory at Gresty Road would temporarily give Rovers a 7-point lead at the top of the table, being already assured of reaching Christmas in top spot, as there were no further league fixtures until Boxing Day. Captain Vaughan Jones considered that the psychological advantage of leading by 7 points would be enormous: 'Imagine how the other clubs will feel when they see the league table on Saturday morning,' he said. After being knocked out of the FA Cup, Rovers were without a fixture the previous weekend, giving several players the chance to recover from flu and rest the little niggles and knocks they carried. However, Ian Alexander failed a late fitness test on a knee damaged in training, which meant a switch to right-back for Steve Yates and a first full senior game of the season for Pete Cawley as partner to Geoff Twentyman. In 1988/89, after six seasons of steady progress, Crewe won promotion to end twenty-five years in the league's basement division, but at the time were hovering above the relegation zone with only four victories. Kenny Swain, their thirty-seven-year-old player-coach, former player for Chelsea, Aston Villa, Portsmouth and European Cup winner with Nottingham Forest, who had scored the goal for Chelsea that knocked Rovers out of the FA Cup in January 1976, was included in the struggling home team.

However, Rovers were in trouble from the 3rd minute when Francis Joseph, making his debut after being signed on loan from Gillingham, scored what at first appeared a good goal only to have it disallowed for what must have been the narrowest of offside decisions. Joseph looked a much sharper player than when Rovers borrowed him from Reading during the 1987/88 season, and he soon brought a reflex save from Brian Parkin, before shaving the goalkeeper's crossbar with a fierce left-foot shot. David Mehew's speedy runs in from the right posed the only threat to Crewe, but Rovers' overall play lacked any real penetration. In the second half another Mehew run from the right led to Dean Greygoose having to make a difficult save as Paul Nixon slid in with a final touch, but he failed to get the right angle on the shot. Crewe took the lead in the 65th minute with a goal from Kenny Swain, his first since joining the Railwaymen eighteen months previously. He shot first-time and it sneaked just inside the far post from an angle on the right, following a Paul Edwards cross from the opposite flank. Falling behind stung Rovers into more purposeful action but the only time they went close to equalising was when Greygoose saved a 25-yard blockbuster from Vaughan Jones, after Andy Reece touched a free-kick to his skipper. Crewe might well have added a second goal in injury time when Fishenden slipped the ball past the advancing Parkin only for Twentyman to clear off the line.

The end of a proud run of 14 league matches without defeat was always going to be a sad occasion, but for it to happen on a cold wet winter's night made it even more depressing. According to Gerry Francis, it was more a matter of Rovers losing the game than Crewe winning it, as 'we showed no urgency until after they scored'. The absence of the injured Ian Alexander was significant, with Steve Yates, hastily recalled to fill the vacancy after injury, clearly short of match fitness and ill-at-ease in an unfamiliar right-back role. But an acute shortage of players left Francis with little choice.

### Tuesday 26 December 1989, Twerton Park

**Bristol Rovers** 0
**Birmingham City** 0
**Half-time**: 0–0
**Attendance**: 6,573
**Referee**: Keith Cooper (Swindon)
**Bristol Rovers**: Parkin, Alexander, Twentyman, Yates, Mehew, Jones, Holloway, Reece, White, Sealy, Nixon. Substitutes: Cawley for Alexander (85 mins), McClean (not used).
**Birmingham City**: Thomas, Atkins, Clarkson, Overson, Matthewson, Frain, Bell, Langley, Gleghorn, Yates, Bailey. Substitutes: Tait for Bailey (68 mins), Peer (not used).

With the Leyland Daf Cup tie with Exeter postponed on Wednesday 20th due to an unfit pitch, the Football League wanted Rovers to play the match on Saturday 23rd – a blank fixture day. However, Gerry Francis was totally against the rearranged game taking place on that date, as he said: 'with 3 major games coming up in seven days, I don't want another one in front of that run'. The decision by the officials at Lytham St Anne's to reschedule the game for Wednesday 17 January thus removed the manager's fears of creating a Christmas fixture pile-up. Dennis Bailey returned to Twerton Park for the all-ticket Boxing Day match, with a Birmingham side sitting just outside the promotion places in 7th spot, and a determination to put one over on his former teammates. Bailey, who had scored ten times for the Midlanders since his £80,000 transfer from Crystal Palace in the summer, spent a highly successful three-month loan spell with Rovers in 1988/89. Following heavy defeats at Rotherham (5–1) and Chester (4–0) earlier in the season, manager Dave Mackay introduced a sweeper system for away games,

Ian Atkins, a future Rovers boss, assuming the libero role.

On a sunny early kick-off (12.30 p.m.) Rovers had three reasonable chances to open the scoring in the opening 25 minutes. First, David Mehew swept the ball wide after Tony Sealy had set up the opening. Then the game's outstanding creative force, Ian Holloway, produced a brilliant burst into the penalty area, but he was foiled by former Rovers teammate, goalkeeper Martin Thomas, who advanced to narrow the angle and then pounced to his left to save. Finally, Holloway advancing down the right won a corner when his shot was blocked by Atkins, but from Andy Reece's corner, Devon White headed wastefully over the crossbar when it appeared easier to score. Within 30 seconds of the restart Rovers came close to taking

Devon White contests the ball with Birmingham's defender Ian Atkins – a future Rovers manager.

the lead. Vaughan Jones centred from the left for Sealy to challenge in the penalty area. The ball came over to Devon White who headed across the area to Mehew in space on the right, who chipped over a shot which Thomas just tipped over the crossbar for a corner.

Tony Sealy battles for the ball during the 0–0 Boxing Day clash with Birmingham City.

Just after the hour Vaughan Jones took a free-kick from just outside the left side of the penalty area and decided to shoot directly for goal, hoping to catch his former teammate in the Birmingham goal unprepared. His direct shot was deflected by the defensive wall and almost crept into the goal at the near post, but Thomas managed to turn it around the post for a corner. Dennis Bailey, the striker Gerry Francis wanted to keep but could not afford after his three-month loan, was ushered off after 68 minutes and replaced by seventeen-year-old Paul Tait. Bailey's failure to manage one shot or pose a single problem to the Third Division's most frugal defence was due to Steve Yates' containment of the striker. The clash between former colleagues simply wasn't a contest, as Yates, Geoff Twentyman, the fit-again Ian Alexander and captain Vaughan Jones at full-back were all magnificent. The defence only looked like being penetrated twice in the second half, but Brian Parkin dived to save from Doug Bell and then with 5 minutes remaining took off to his left to brilliantly touch a John Frain header round the post after good work from Tait.

A late Birmingham goal would have been tough on Rovers, who monopolised much of the game but faltered against a side playing with a sweeper, for whom Ian Atkins played the role admirably. Rovers had successfully overcome sweeper defences earlier in the season, but against Notts County and Preston, goals had come early. Gerry Francis was far from downhearted with the loss of two home points, preferring to look at the positive factors. 'After playing only one game in over three weeks, the players have retained match fitness,' said the manager, and significantly Rovers' defence had kept their 11th clean sheet in 20 league games.

## Saturday 30 December 1989, Twerton Park

**Bristol Rovers** 2 – Nixon, Vickers (own goal)
**Tranmere Rovers** 0
**Half-time**: 0–0
**Attendance**: 6,821
**Referee**: Ian Hemley (Ampthill)
**Bristol Rovers**: Parkin, Alexander, Twentyman, Yates, Mehew, Jones, Holloway, Reece, White, Sealy, Nixon. Substitutes: McClean for Nixon (87 mins), Cawley (not used).
**Tranmere Rovers**: Nixon, Thomas, Vickers, Hughes, Higgins, McCarrick, Fairclough, Harvey, Martindale, Steel, Muir. Substitutes: Malkin for Harvey (45 minutes), Bishop for Fairclough (50 mins).

Gerry Francis was reported as being interested in bringing Steve White back to Rovers for a third spell, but despite the club banking £1.5 million from the sale of Nigel Martyn and Gary Penrice, Rovers' board imposed limitations on the amount the club could spend in the transfer market. Swindon Town had also made it clear that they wanted more than the £70,000 offered for the striker. Brian Parkin had clearly demonstrated his value since joining Rovers as only 2 goals had gone past the twenty-four-year-old in 5 games.

Tranmere Rovers, lying fifth in the table, 4 points behind the Pirates, took to the Twerton pitch to a cheer from the crowd as the stadium announcer, Keith Valle, told them: 'Any side that can beat Bristol City 6–0 deserves a round of applause'; a result they achieved in September at Prenton Park. It was soon evident that Bristol Rovers would not get the City treatment, for Tranmere strung five at the back using one-time Eastville player Mark Hughes as their sweeper. They were by no means entirely negative, but the spaces in midfield meant Rovers were able to do most of the attacking. Early on, David Mehew squandered a chance with a weak shot, after Devon White knocked the ball down to him, but he found no power as he met it awkwardly. Andy Reece, who provided strong midfield back-up for Ian Holloway, also put in a soft finish when presented with a scoring opportunity. Ian Alexander, showing sharpness at right-back, put in a deep cross which Reece got well behind, only to see his shot palmed over the crossbar by Eric Nixon for one of the game's few corners.

Tony Sealy causes problems for the Tranmere Rovers defence with goalkeeper Eric Nixon grounded.

Rovers almost gave a goal away when Tranmere left-back Mark McCarrick was allowed to burst through when clearly offside, which referee Ian Hemley and a linesman failed to spot. There was another anxious moment when the referee gave Tranmere a free-kick, dangerously near goal, after Vaughan Jones had appeared to have won the ball cleanly in a tackle, but fortunately the shot came to nothing. One-time Liverpool forward David Fairclough landed heavily on his shoulder as he tried to avoid tackles from Jones and Twentyman, realising that it was a bad knock Twentyman immediately kicked the ball into touch, so the referee could stop play. But for Fairclough the game was over and he was stretchered off with a suspected broken collar bone. A far-post volley from the left by Paul Nixon gave the home side their breakthrough after 66 minutes. It was conjured up for him by the heads of Twentyman and Devon White, who back-headed an intelligent long throw to the near post from Vaughan Jones.

Three minutes later, with Rovers chasing a second goal Paul Nixon hammered in a shot, following good work from Devon White, which Tranmere defender Steve Vickers could only slice into his own goal off his outstretched left leg.

Rovers' protective shield with the best goals-against record in the country saw to it that Brian Parkin did not have to make one direct save against their promotion rivals, as the Pirates held on to 2nd place in Division Three.

Following a Vaughan Jones throw-in, Paul Nixon opens the scoring against 5th placed Tranmere Rovers.

## Monday 1 January 1990, Millmoor, Rotherham

**Rotherham United** 3 – Evans, Hazel, Williamson (penalty)
**Bristol Rovers** 2 – Mehew, Holloway (penalty)
**Half-time**: 1–1
**Attendance**: 7,750
**Referee**: Terry Lunt (Ashton-in-Makerfield)
**Rotherham United**: Mercer, Barnsley, Robinson, Grealish, Russell, Scott, Buckley, Goodwin, Williamson, Evans, Hazel. Substitutes: Pepper for Buckley (14 mins), Goater (not used).
**Bristol Rovers**: Parkin, Alexander, Twentyman, Yates, Mehew, Jones, Holloway, Reece, White, Sealy, Hazel. Substitutes: McClean for Hazel (half-time), Cawley (not used).

As 1990 began Rovers, defeated only twice in the league all season, were in 2nd place with 41 points, their steel town New Year's Day opponents four places below them with 7 points fewer. Rovers' only team change from their final victory of 1989 against Tranmere Rovers was the inclusion of Ian Hazel for the injured Paul Nixon. Rotherham, with the best home record in the Third Division, included the former Republic of Ireland midfielder Tony Grealish, and Shaun Goater, a future Bristol City striker, as a substitute.

Kicking off in relentless rain, with a chilling wind and on a greasy pitch, Rotherham took the lead in the 14th minute with a well-headed goal from Stewart Evans. However, the build-up to the goal involved an incident which fired the passions of both sets of players. As John Buckley crossed from the left, his right leg was caught by an Ian Alexander tackle, which resulted in the winger being stretchered off and taken straight to hospital. Running feuds were then allowed to continue by referee Terry Lunt, who at one time seemed in danger of losing control of the situation. To the delight of the massed hordes of visiting Rovers fans, David Mehew's 10th goal of the season put Rovers back level a minute from half-time. The sharply taken strike was hooked in after an Andy Reece corner from the right had been flicked on by the head of Devon White.

Two minutes after the restart Christian McClean, who took over as substitute for the injured Ian Hazel at the interval, was tripped moving into the Rotherham penalty area by Billy Russell. Ian Holloway sent goalkeeper Billy Mercer the wrong way with his spot-kick and Rovers were ahead – but not for long. Ten minutes later, a deflection off Tony Grealish dropped nicely for Des Hazel, who was allowed too much freedom by the Rovers' defence and tucked a low

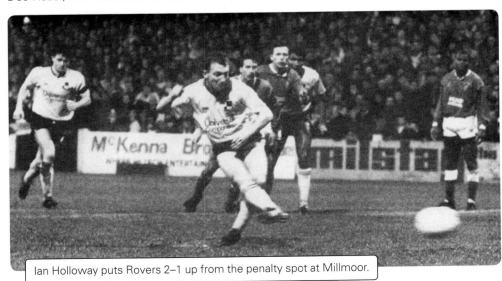

Ian Holloway puts Rovers 2–1 up from the penalty spot at Millmoor.

drive from the right just inside Brian Parkin's far post. Parkin then denied Evans a second goal with a reflex save, to turn a close-range header over the bar.

Then, in the 67th minute, a linesman signalled a handling offence against Steve Yates as the ball bounced up and struck his arm. Bobby Williamson took advantage of what seemed a harsh penalty decision to score past Brian Parkin and give the Millers the lead. Rovers had cause to complain of further rough justice 5 minutes from the end when a Tony Sealy header from Vaughan Jones free-kick was deflected away from danger by a defender's arm. Rovers had a last-gasp opportunity to rescue something from the game when David Mehew was through in the 88th minute with only the goalkeeper to beat, but nineteen-year-old Mercer, making his league debut, smothered the ball before holding it at the second attempt – and the 3 points remained with Rotherham.

In front of Millmoor's biggest league gate of the season, Rotherham maintained their home three-goal-a-match average against a side with the best defensive record in the division and moved into fourth place. Rovers, who suffered their third league defeat of the season, had lost for the first time after leading in a match. It was also the first time in the season they had 3 goals put past them.

## Saturday 13 January 1990. Twerton Park

**Bristol Rovers** 1 – Twentyman
**Mansfield Town** 1 – Leishman
**Half-time**: 1–0
**Attendance**: 5,339
**Referee**: Paul Alcock (South Merstham)
**Bristol Rovers**: Parkin, Alexander, Twentyman, Yates, Mehew, Jones, Holloway, Reece, White, Sealy, Nixon. Substitutes: Purnell for Sealy (70 mins), Cawley (not used).
**Mansfield Town**: Beasley, Murray, Prindiville, Christie, Foster, Smalley, Kent, Hunt, Wilkinson, Charles, Kearney. Substitutes: Chambers for Charles (40 mins), Leishman for Smalley (74 mins).

After initially turning down a permanent move from Crystal Palace to Rovers, Brian Parkin signed for the Pirates on the Thursday before the Mansfield game, thus averting a goalkeeping crisis for Gerry Francis. After two days of negotiations he agreed to sign a two-and-a-half-year contract. During the previous weeks Francis had been searching for two or three signings as Rovers sought to improve on three draws in their last 5 league games at Twerton Park. Rovers also welcomed back Phil Purnell to the squad for the first time since recovering from injury. The winger made his first playing appearance for seven months in the reserves against Torquay at Keynsham on the 4 January, scoring in the 4–0 win. Mansfield's fortunes had plummeted since Rovers sneaked a 1–0 win at Field Mill at the start of the season, and the Stags found themselves second from bottom with just six wins in 22 games. They had shown they were capable of shock results after beating high-flying Rotherham 3–1 on Boxing Day, but were without leading striker Ian Stringfellow.

Rovers missed two opportunities in the opening minutes when both David Mehew and Tony Sealy squandered good scoring chances. Vaughan Jones dropped a free-kick at Mehew's feet but he hesitated over what should have been a solid strike, while Sealy was caught on the wrong foot when Paul Nixon crossed to him. There was little rhythm or fluency to Rovers' game at the start of the match, coming off second best in the air and giving the ball away. However, the tide started to turn as Holloway let go a 25-yard shot, but it was too straight and went directly to the goalkeeper. The deadlock was broken after 26 minutes by Geoff Twentyman, coming up for Rovers' fourth corner of the game to give his team the lead. Goalkeeper Andy Beasley moved too early for Reece's well-struck corner from the right which passed embarrassingly over his head to Twentyman, who outjumped a defender to nod in from a couple of yards.

Geoff Twentyman heads Rovers into the lead after 26 minutes against Mansfield Town with his second goal of the season.

Holloway, on a speedy break from a Mehew through ball, beat the offside trap with a great run but his final ball was too easily intercepted by the experienced George Foster, Town's player-manager, who headed away. Alexander inadvertently helped Mansfield early in the second half by hitting a 25-yard ball back towards his own goalkeeper without looking up, which fell into the path of Trevor Christie. However, the striker missed his chance but it was still a boost to their morale. Beasley made a point-blank save from a Sealy volley which the keeper stopped by instinct, and he stuck out a foot while diving in the opposite direction to deny Reece a goal.

The introduction of Phil Purnell, to a big cheer from the crowd, for the final 21 minutes on the left flank, allowed Nixon to move inside at Sealy's expense. But it was a gamble that failed, as the winger, unsurprisingly, was not match-fit for his first outing of the season and had few touches of the ball. After holding a narrow lead for an hour complacency crept into Rovers' game, and with the introduction of Mansfield's substitute, Graham Leishman, the Stags found a new confidence. The young reserve striker replaced defender Mark Smalley, a former Rovers loan signing, and with his first effort Leishman hit a crisp shot on the turn, which drew an arching near-post save from Parkin and won one of Mansfield's two corners. With barely 5 minutes left Trevor Christie crossed and Leishman, fed by Steve Wilkinson, slotted the ball beneath Parkin's body to score his first goal of the season.

This was a Rovers performance well below the standard expected by Gerry Francis, with the dejected manager complaining that, 'The game should have been over by half-time. The 'keeper made good saves, but we missed so many chances.' Nineteen goal attempts – 11 on target – were revealing match facts as Mansfield's late gamble ended a miserable run of eight away defeats, and Rovers failed to beat a side twenty-one places lower than them after dominating the first 70 minutes. Francis warned that Rovers' promotion run would fade unless he could get more players to augment his squad.

## 13 JANUARY 1990

|  | P | W | D | L | F | A | Pts |
|---|---|---|---|---|---|---|---|
| Bristol City | 23 | 13 | 5 | 5 | 32 | 20 | 44 |
| Notts County | 24 | 12 | 7 | 5 | 36 | 25 | 43 |
| BRISTOL ROVERS | 23 | 11 | 9 | 3 | 31 | 17 | 42 |
| Bury | 24 | 11 | 6 | 7 | 41 | 31 | 39 |
| Bolton Wanderers | 23 | 10 | 9 | 4 | 35 | 25 | 39 |
| Huddersfield Town | 23 | 10 | 9 | 4 | 32 | 27 | 39 |
| Rotherham United | 24 | 10 | 7 | 7 | 47 | 31 | 37 |

## Wednesday 17 January 1990, Twerton Park
## Leyland Daf Cup Southern Preliminary Round Group 2

**Bristol Rovers** 3 – Holloway (penalty), Sealy, Mehew
**Exeter City** 0
**Half-time**: 1–0
**Attendance**: 3,136
**Referee**: Keith Burge (Tonypandy)
**Bristol Rovers**: Parkin, Alexander, Twentyman, Yates, Mehew, Jones, Holloway, Reece, McClean, Sealy, Nixon. Substitutes: Browning for Nixon (62 mins), Cawley (not used).
**Exeter City**: Walter, Hiley, Benjamin, Rogers, Heath, Cooper, Eshelby, Batty, McDermott, Locke, Frankland. Substitutes: Bailey for Locke (67 mins), Annunziata (not used).

Terry Cooper, manager of the in-form Fourth Division leaders, decided to rest a number of first team regulars including Darren Rowbotham, the twenty-four-goal leading marksman and his striking partner, former Bristol City favourite, Steve Neville. He defended his decision, stating that his team had been involved in a lot of football in the previous months and that he did not want to risk anyone who was not fully fit. But the former player and

Ian Holloway scores Rovers' opening goal from the penalty spot after 10 minutes against Exeter City.

Tony Sealy slots in Rovers' second Leyland Daf Cup goal after Exeter goalkeeper Walter could only palm out Mehew's initial shot.

manager of both Bristol clubs denied that he was not taking the competition seriously or deliberately resting players for the league visit to Doncaster on Saturday. Rovers on the other hand fielded the strongest available team, with Christian McClean staking a claim for a regular place. The big striker was set to make his fourth appearance of the season because Devon White was suspended for 2 matches. Rovers, who drew at Torquay in November, would qualify for a home match in the first round by winning against the Grecians, with a point enough to see them through.

Rovers started promisingly as they tore into the visitors' makeshift defence with David Mehew going close on three occasions inside the first 7 minutes. A clever near-post flick instinctively saved by Walter in the second minute was the nearest to scoring, but they deservedly went ahead in the 10th minute through an Ian Holloway penalty. The awarding of the spot-kick was a controversial decision by referee Keith Burge who ruled that former Bristol City defender Lee Rogers had brought down Paul Nixon just inside the penalty area. Holloway stepped up to side-foot the ball past goalkeeper Dave Walter's left hand. Chances continued to come Rovers way with Walter keeping the home side at bay, and a shot from Mehew was diverted off the line by a defender seconds before half-time.

After the interval Gerry Francis gave eighteen-year-old Marcus Browning his senior debut; he replaced Paul Nixon, and the youngster showed some nice touches during his 30-minute appearance. After 81 minutes, just when it looked as though Rovers had settled for the one goal, Mehew surged forward from midfield to shoot low to Walter's right. The goalkeeper could only palm the ball out to Tony Sealy who slotted it into the goal. Mehew added a third goal 5 minutes later. Following a Reece cross, Marcus Browning and McClean worked the ball down the left, leaving Sealy to set up a simple 11th goal of the season for Rovers' leading goalscorer.

Thus Rovers progressed to the knock-out stage of the competition and by finishing top of the group earned a home tie – against Gillingham – a week later, with Torquay eliminated.

## Leyland Daf Cup Southern Preliminary Round Group 2 – Final Table

|  | P | W | D | L | F | A | Pts |
|---|---|---|---|---|---|---|---|
| BRISTOL ROVERS | 2 | 1 | 1 | 0 | 4 | 1 | 4 |
| Exeter City | 2 | 1 | 0 | 1 | 2 | 3 | 3 |
| Torquay United | 2 | 0 | 1 | 1 | 1 | 3 | 1 |

## Saturday 20 January 1990, Griffin Park, Brentford

Brentford 2 – Ratcliffe, Cadette
Bristol Rovers 1 – McClean
Half-time: 0–0
Attendance: 7,414
Referee: David Axcell (Southend-on-Sea)
**Brentford**: Parks, Ratcliffe, Stanislaus, Bates, Evans, Cockram, Jones, May, Holdsworth, Cadette, Smillie. Substitutes: Buttigieg (not used), Godfrey (not used).
**Bristol Rovers**: Parkin, Alexander, Twentyman, Yates, Mehew, Jones, Holloway, Reece, McClean, Sealy, Nixon. Substitutes: Purnell for Nixon (88 mins), Cawley (not used).

Brentford's two previous home games had both resulted in 4-goal victories (4–0 against Walsall and 4–2 over Rotherham United), but the London side could still be found languishing just above the relegation places. With Devon White still suspended, Christian McClean again deputised, the only doubt being Paul Nixon who strained a calf muscle in the midweek match. Ian Willmott and Marcus Browning were standing by, but Gerry Francis was hopeful to field an unchanged side.

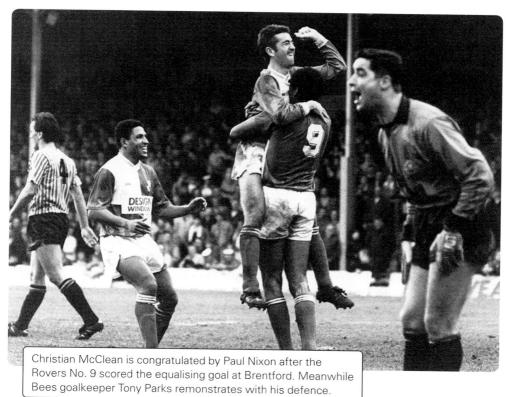

Christian McClean is congratulated by Paul Nixon after the Rovers No. 9 scored the equalising goal at Brentford. Meanwhile Bees goalkeeper Tony Parks remonstrates with his defence.

Geoff Twentyman is thwarted by the Brentford defence as he attempts to score from a corner.

Brentford had the best of the early exchanges in the first 10 minutes as Rovers survived a series of three corners in a minute, but then they showed how dangerous they could be on the break when Tony Sealy got past Terry Evans and brought a fingertip save from Tony Parks in the Bees' goal. The best chance came on the half hour when Christian McClean won the ball in the Brentford penalty area, but Andy Reece was just wide with a shot from 20 yards. A flying Paul Nixon header was held by Parks as Holloway, Mehew and Reece began to dominate the midfield, and former Brentford man Holloway had Evans at full stretch to cut out a through pass with McClean bearing down on goal. Six minutes before half-time, Brentford came closest to breaking the deadlock when a Neil Smillie shot from a Ratcliffe low cross, was cleared off the line by Geoff Twentyman. Dean Holdsworth then scraped the Rovers crossbar from 20 yards. Ian Holloway set up Paul Nixon late in the first half and only an outstanding tackle by Jamie Bates prevented a goal. Brentford took the lead after 51 minutes with a low left-foot shot by Simon Ratcliffe from 10 yards out through a crowd of players, after Rovers' defence had made several abortive attempts to clear a corner from Neil Smillie; the ball was deflected by Twentyman's boot. Christian McClean put Rovers back in the game almost immediately with a neat side-footed shot, following Reece's angled header, which squeezed between goalkeeper Parks and the far post for a 53rd-minute equaliser and his first goal of the season.

A few minutes later the striker had the vociferous Rovers travelling contingent roaring again when he was put through by Tony Sealy, but McClean lifted a right-foot 18-yard shot into the crowd, when his left foot seemed the more appropriate choice. With 6 minutes remaining and a draw looking the likeliest result, McClean attempted a back-heel while hemmed in by the touchline, lost the ball, and in attempting to win it back was penalised and lectured for a clumsy trip. Helping back in defence the 6ft 4in striker was outjumped on the edge of the penalty area by Terry Evans as they contested former Rovers player Allan Cockram's free-kick. Evan's header found Richard Cadette, who was given too much room by Steve Yates and his shot from 8 yards struck the diving Brian Parkin's wrist, bounced up, hit the keeper on the back of the head before rolling over the line. The defeat left Rovers just hanging on to third place after a third consecutive league defeat away from home.

Praise for the noisy Bristol Rovers fans at Griffin Park came from an unusual source. Brentford boss Steve Perryman, who stood at the back of the stand and couldn't fail to hear the blue chorus, thanked them for keeping his Bees busy: 'I thought the crowd was doing more for them, but they still created a good atmosphere for us to play in even if their voices were not in our favour.' He also felt that Rovers could keep up their challenge without improving the squad as they were so well organised and solid at the back. All that was wrong with Rovers was the indifferent finishing – their attitude and application was outstanding.

## Wednesday 24 January 1990, Twerton Park
## Leyland Daf Cup Southern First Round

**Bristol Rovers** 1 – Nixon
**Gillingham** 0
**Half-time**: 1–0
**Attendance**: 2,724
**Referee**: Keren Barratt (Coventry)
**Bristol Rovers**: Parkin, Alexander, Twentyman, Yates, Mehew, Jones, Holloway, Reece, White, Sealy, Purnell. Substitutes: Nixon for Sealy (36 mins), Cawley (not used).
**Gillingham**: Lim, Haylock, Manuel, Pulis, Walker, Palmer, Docker, O'Shea, Gavin, Heritage, O'Connor. Substitutes: Eeles for Pulis (half-time), Lovell for Gavin (69 mins).

Two former Rovers favourites posed a major threat to Gerry Francis' plans to take his 1990 line-up all the way to Wembley. Mark O'Connor and Tony Pulis, both arriving at Priestfield Road via Bournemouth, linked up in Gillingham's midfield; O'Connor having made a major impact since joining the Fourth Division club for £65,000, and Pulis adding aggression to the side after recovering from a long-term thigh injury. Francis gave Phil Purnell his first full game of the season, the left-winger having played 2 reserve games and made 2 brief first-team appearances as substitute since having a knee operation in the summer. Francis acknowledged that the wingman wasn't exactly fit, but felt that, 'he might as well attempt to reach fitness in the first team rather than the reserves'. Marcus Browning, the first year professional who had scored consistently in the reserves, was also included in the squad.

The home side went close to grabbing an early lead when Reece drilled a low shot wide of the goal from the edge of the box. Mark O'Connor released Gillingham's first positive strike, a good effort from more than 20 yards, which Brian Parkin sprang to save. A header from Peter Heritage produced the Gills' third corner in the opening minutes and then captain Alan Walker appeared in the penalty area unannounced to let fly with a volley that Parkin was pleased to beat away. For Rovers, Devon White got in a header which was held by Lim, while Sealy hit another shot wide before these two attackers combined to fashion an even better 28th-minute opportunity. White took a return pass from Sealy, but from a favourable position sliced his

Phil Purnell attempts to break through the Gillingham defence in his first full game of the season.

Substitute Paul Nixon scores Rovers' winning goal against Gillingham in the Leyland Daf Cup tie.

attempt past the post. Parkin then made a save, springing full length to keep out Heritage's header from a centre by Pat Gavin. Substitute Paul Nixon got his chance after 36 minutes, replacing Tony Sealy who failed to return after going off to have five stitches inserted in a cut to his forehead. It was Nixon who registered the decisive goal 5 minutes after taking the field. The goalscoring move stemmed from a deep cross by Ian Alexander, who had been allowed a free run down the right. Devon White nodded down to Andy Reece, who was felled as he raced across goalkeeper Harvey Lim. It was a clear penalty but the ball ran for Nixon to lash home before the referee could signal a spot-kick.

Tony Pulis, who was cautioned for a 31st-minute tackle on Ian Holloway, did not come out for the second half, his absence caused by a hamstring strain. Moments after making a hash of a cross from a free position, Haylock then provided Gillingham with their best chance of an equaliser. His ball played in from the right, with Rovers appealing for an offside decision, left full-back Billy Manuel with just Parkin to beat, but although his lob easily cleared the goalkeeper it cleared the crossbar as well. Twice in as many minutes Phil Purnell went close to increasing Rovers' slim advantage. He first cut in from the left to let go a fiercely driven cross-shot that Lim went down to save well and then, from a similar position, sent a cleverly chipped shot floating marginally wide. Lim came out a long way in an effort to reach an 80th-minute cross swung over from Reece, but failed to reach the ball leaving Devon White with an open goal, but the 'keeper was spared further embarrassment as White sent his header bouncing wide of the empty net. As the clock ticked towards the final minute, second Gills substitute Lovell went close to plunging the tie into extra time, but his shot was deflected wide. So, as the old football cliché goes Gillingham were now free to concentrate on the league … and the Kent Senior Cup.

### Sunday 28 January 1990, Twerton Park

**Bristol Rovers** 1 – Reece
**Bolton Wanderers** 1 – Philliskirk
**Half-time**: 1–0
**Attendance**: 7,722
**Referee**: John Lloyd (Wrexham)
**Bristol Rovers**: Parkin, Alexander, Twentyman, Yates, Mehew, Jones, Holloway, Reece, White, Nixon, Purnell. Substitutes: Browning for Nixon (88 mins), Cawley (not used).
**Bolton Wanderers**: Felgate, Brown, Cowdrill, Comstive, Crombie, Came, Storer, Thompson, Reeves, Philliskirk, Darby. Substitutes: Henshaw (not used), Savage (not used).

A win against promotion rivals Bolton was vital if Rovers with 42 points – 5 fewer than new leaders Bristol City – wanted to stay in touch with their neighbours. Bolton, unbeaten in 7 consecutive league and cup matches, were also on 42 points but one place behind Rovers in third because their goal difference was one less. Phil Neal's team were without central defender Mark Winstanley who had a back injury, whilst Rovers delayed selection for a late fitness test on Tony Sealy, who had five stitches in a head wound suffered against Gillingham.

The promise of Phil Neal to show regard for – but no fear of – Rovers' proud home record was borne out as early as the 6th minute when Tony Philliskirk headed just wide from Paul Comstive's left-wing cross. Then it needed an excellent tackle by Steve Yates to halt Stuart Storer's progress after the Bolton winger had sprinted past Vaughan Jones. After that Rovers took charge of the game, but Felgate's agility denied Devon White twice and then Andy Reece. And it was Reece who broke the deadlock after 38 minutes; following good work by Paul Nixon, David Mehew centred and Reece hit his shot on the turn past Felgate.

Bolton drew level 5 minutes into the second half with Tony Philliskirk's measured left-footed drive, after Comstive had flicked on Barry Cowdrill's cross, for his 15th goal of the season. Comstive cleared off Bolton's line from Paul Nixon as Rovers rallied, but Devon White wasted the best chance of sealing a win when he tapped a perfectly laid ball from Ian Holloway too far ahead of himself. Goalkeeper Dave Felgate rushed out and White's strike flew inches past the wrong side of the post. Eighteen-year-old Marcus Browning was sent on as a substitute for Paul Nixon 2 minutes from the end, for his first league appearance, in an attempt to inspire a dramatic Rovers winner. He almost did it with a burst down the left, but White headed his centre narrowly wide of the near post seconds before the end.

The match was a marvellous advertisement for Third Division football, played between two teams with the credentials to remain among the leading pack. Rovers really needed 3 points in a match watched by Rovers' biggest home crowd of the season, the size of which gave the club serious consideration about staging more Sunday afternoon matches. Rovers produced three times as many goal attempts as their opponents, but a fifth home draw in 7 games

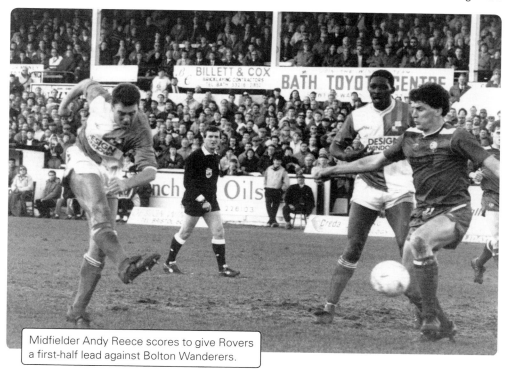

Midfielder Andy Reece scores to give Rovers a first-half lead against Bolton Wanderers.

since Penrice was sold – he was in the crowd at Twerton – showed how badly Rovers needed a consistent goalscorer. Francis succinctly summed up, 'We played well and it was a draw. What more can you say?'

## Tuesday 6 February 1990, Griffin Park, Brentford
## Leyland Daf Cup Southern Quarter Final

**Brentford** 2 – Smillie, Holdsworth
**Bristol Rovers** 2 – Holloway (penalty), Saunders
Bristol Rovers won 4–3 on penalties after extra time. Rovers' scorers: Holloway, Jones, Purnell, Twentyman. Brentford scorers: Cockram, Holdsworth, Stanislaus.
**Half-time**: 1–0
**Attendance**: 4,409
**Referee**: Keith Cooper (Pontypridd)
**Brentford**: Parks, Ratcliffe, Stanislaus, Cousins, Bates, Cockram, Jones, May, Holdsworth, Cadette, Smillie. Substitutes: Buttigieg for Cousins (105 mins), Blissett for Cadette (95 mins).
**Bristol Rovers**: Parkin, Alexander, Twentyman, Yates, Mehew, Jones, Holloway, Reece, White, Saunders, Purnell. Substitutes: Byrne for Mehew (111 mins), Willmott (not used).

Rovers had ten days' preparation for this rearranged match following the postponement of 2 games, the original Leyland Daf Cup tie scheduled for the 30 January, and the Bristol derby at Twerton Park called off on 3 February due to a waterlogged pitch. During this period manager Gerry Francis was active in the transfer market and after failing in a £100,000 bid to bring Birmingham City marksman Dennis Bailey back to Rovers, Francis turned to other targets. He landed two new players, Stoke City's Carl Saunders, signed for £70,000 and right-winger David Byrne from Plymouth Argyle, who joined initially on a month's loan. Both were named in Rovers' squad, the team being selected an hour before kick-off.

The visitors, beaten by their opponents in the league two weeks earlier, went behind from the first meaningful break of the match in the 8th minute. Neil Smillie received the ball well inside his own half as Andy Reece failed to cut out a clearance and set off for goal. Ian Alexander tried to check his progress but Smillie beat the late challenge and kept his balance before striking a left foot shot from the edge of the area. Brian Parkin got a hand to it but the ball crept into the far corner of the net. Rovers responded 4 minutes later when Twentyman headed Vaughan Jones' centre inches wide, and as they bombarded the Brentford goal, White, Alexander and debutant Carl Saunders all fired wide. Rovers levelled matters from their first shot on target when a cross from Phil Purnell, a constant threat on the left-wing, was handled in the box by Simon Ratcliffe as Devon White closed in. Ian Holloway converted the penalty in the 36th minute sending Tony Parks the wrong way. Just before the break White combined with Saunders and hammered a first-time shot inches over Parks' crossbar. Dean Holdsworth missed a great chance for the Bees from close range in the 61st minute, but Rovers' command of the game continued after the interval and only good Brentford defending prevented another goal. That did not come until extra time and the 100th-minute when Saunders marked his debut with a goal. Vaughan Jones' free-kick was nodded on by Devon White to Saunders who turned on the edge of the penalty area and fired his shot low into the right corner of the goal. But a missed punch by Parkin allowed Holdsworth to beat Steve Yates and head Ratcliffe's through ball home in the dying seconds, taking the game to a penalty shoot-out.

First Allan Cockram netted for Brentford and Ian Holloway levelled. Gary Blissett fired over and Vaughan Jones sent Parks the wrong way to put Rovers 2–1 up. Holdsworth and Phil Purnell both netted and Bees full-back Roger Stanislaus tied it up at 3–3. Rovers needed to convert their last two penalties to be certain of victory but dramatically Andy Reece's shot was saved by Parks, who was Tottenham's spot-kick hero in the 1984 UEFA Cup final.

Further drama ensued as Brian Parkin saved Maltese international John Buttigieg's shot, which left Geoff Twentyman with the chance to put Rovers through to the Southern Area Semi-Final of the competition. Reminded by the referee that he 'needed to put it in for the winner', it helped Twentyman concentrate on the spot-kick, as having missed a crucial penalty four seasons earlier, he had not taken one since – not even in training. He sent Parks the wrong way and the Rovers players charged towards their ecstatic fans to join in the celebrations. However, the action wasn't quite over for the evening as police were called to the Post House Hotel at Heathrow, where Rovers' team bus had stopped en route for home, to interview manager Gerry Francis and Paul Nixon who had had a disagreement about the player's non-selection for the cup-tie.

## Saturday 10 February 1990, Deepdale, Preston

**Preston North End** 0
**Bristol Rovers** 1 – Mehew
**Half-time**: 0–0
**Attendance**: 5,956
**Referee**: Stephen Lodge (Barnsley)
**Preston North End**: Stowell, Williams, Swann, McIlroy, Flynn, Wrightson, Mooney, Greenwood, Joyce, Shaw, Harper. Substitutes: Bogie (not used), Hughes (not used).
**Bristol Rovers**: Parkin, Alexander, Twentyman, Yates, Mehew, Jones, Holloway, Reece, White, Saunders, Purnell. Substitutes: Byrne for Purnell (72 mins), Willmott (not used).

Rovers trained at Bristol University's Coombe Dingle ground on Thursday to get the feel of playing on an artificial pitch as they prepared to visit Preston North End, one of four league clubs playing home matches on a 'plastic' pitch. Vaughan Jones, who played against Brentford with a heavily bandaged left ankle, missed training to rest the injury. Gerry Francis felt that the home side had a definite advantage playing on the pitch, but his focus was on getting Rovers' first league win of the year at Preston. The Pirates last won a league game on 30 December, since then the side had been held to draws at home by Mansfield and Bolton, and lost at Rotherham and Brentford. During December and January Rovers had obtained only 9 league points from a possible 24. Former Northern Ireland international Sammy McIlroy was due to make his Preston debut against Rovers, the thirty-four-year old ex-Manchester United midfielder joined the Deepdale club as player-coach on a free transfer from Bury. Preston had also signed former England international Frank Worthington as a part-time coach.

Rovers quickly settled on Preston's artificial pitch and in the opening minutes went close to scoring. A free-kick by Vaughan Jones was helped on by Geoff Twentyman but Mike Stowell – on loan from Everton – came back quickly to save as Mehew tried to reach the ball. After 10 minutes another Jones free-kick was flicked on by White, and Carl Saunders, making his league debut for the Pirates, was a whisker away from touching in as Gary Swann got a toe to the ball to clear. Twentyman was booked for a late tackle on Steve Harper as Preston staged a 10 minute onslaught on Rovers' goal, winning four quick corners but the defence held firm and Parkin pulled off a great stop, racing off his line to smother the ball as striker Greenwood raced unchallenged into the box. Rovers continued to press and after 22 minutes Andy Reece delivered a neat ball into the box and full-back Neil Williams had to be in quickly to clear as Saunders raced in. Reece then floated a corner from the right and Twentyman, playing against his former club, was unlucky in powering a header straight at Stowell who held it cleanly on his line.

The second half restart was delayed for 35 minutes when home fans staged a sit-in in a section of the Town End stand without a safety certificate, but the delay affected Preston most and Rovers, who had been the better team in the first half, managed to keep their composure on the restart and took the lead they deserved on the hour. From Andy Reece's corner Devon White beat the home 'keeper to the ball in the air and David Mehew, on the edge of the six-yard area, fired in a shot which Stowell failed to hold. Mehew smacked the rebound into the back of the net. The lead was threatened within 3 minutes when Nigel Greenwood slipped past Twentyman, but Parkin was off his goal line to end the danger with a spreading save. Brian Mooney hit a shot on the run which was well saved by Parkin before Rovers replaced Phil Purnell with David Byrne who quickly worried Preston with his speed. Near the end it was Rovers pushing for another goal. Byrne had Stowell scrambling to save a 25-yard ground shot, and Holloway turned neatly after being set up by White but the goalkeeper did well to get down pushing his shot for a corner. Holloway was tripped in the penalty area by Williams 6 minutes from time but play was waved on.

Rovers were clearly steeling themselves for the challenge to regain the Third Division leadership from Bristol City. The team's single-mindedness was demonstrated at Deepdale, where their first league victory of 1990 was achieved despite the most unsettling of circumstances – Preston's artificial pitch, regular squalls making conditions difficult, and a 35-minute unexpected interval.

### Sunday 18 February 1990, Twerton Park

**Bristol Rovers** 2 – Saunders 2
**Walsall** 0
Half-time: 1–0
Attendance: 6,223
Referee: Paul Harrison (Oldham)
**Bristol Rovers**: Parkin, Alexander, Twentyman, Yates, Mehew, Jones, Holloway, Reece, White, Saunders, Purnell. Substitutes: Byrne for Mehew (82 mins), Willmott (not used).
**Walsall**: Barber, Dornan, Whitehouse, Forbes, Skipper, Taylor, Goodwin, Kelly, Rimmer, Bertschin, Thorpe. Substitutes: Saville for Bertschin (75 mins), Hart (not used).

On-loan winger David Byrne, from Plymouth Argyle, takes on the Walsall defence at Twerton Park.

New signing Carl Saunders cracks his second goal of the match against Walsall on his Twerton Park debut.

Rovers' home fixture with bottom club Walsall was switched to Sunday as Bristol City were at home to Cambridge United in the fifth round of the FA Cup on the Saturday. Walsall, although propping up the foot of the table had done better away from home and conceded fewer away goals than high-riding clubs like Huddersfield and Rotherham. It was Rovers' first chance to show the home fans new signings Carl Saunders and David Byrne. Christian McClean's unrest about his potential for first-team appearances, following the arrival of the two new forwards, resulted in the striker requesting a transfer, which was duly turned down. 'I understand Christian wanting to play in the first-team but you have got to have a strong squad and the six or seven not playing are equally important', commented Gerry Francis on his reason for the transfer refusal. The view was reinforced by assistant manager Kenny Hibbitt, 'These two new players have strengthened the squad which was much needed, not only because of the heavy schedule ahead but also to give the present squad a boost'.

Carl Saunders made an immediate impact as he and Devon White tormented the Walsall defence from the start. In the 9th minute he shot wide following a mix-up in the Saddlers' back-four and 20 minutes later Mehew and White worked the ball to the debutant, but again he was wide of the target. Having squandered two good chances, Saunders broke the deadlock in the 31st minute. He turned his marker, Andy Dornan, and forced a sharp save from goalkeeper Fred Barber. From the resulting corner the £70,000 signing from Stoke scored from close range after Holloway's corner-kick was knocked down by Mehew. The twenty-five-year-old Midlander was then put clear in first-half injury time only to be foiled by Barber's alertness as the 'keeper came quickly out of the penalty area to clear with his feet.

At 1–0 early in the second half, it needed good recovery work by David Mehew to deny Stuart Rimmer a close-range shot after Alex Taylor's pass had penetrated the home defence. Rimmer again narrowly failed to equalise when he shot onto the base of a post after goalkeeper Fred Barber's clearance was flicked on by the head of Keith Bertschin. Later nippy winger Adrian Thorpe steered the ball wide from a good position and then shot straight at Brian Parkin. A drive over, another shot wide and one straight at Barber let Walsall off the hook until the second goal arrived, 7 minutes from time, from a well-rehearsed set-piece.

Vaughan Jones' free-kick was headed on by White for Saunders to beat Whitehouse to the ball and volley past Barber. Twerton fans' first glimpse of their club's other newcomer David Byrne suggested he too would be an asset during the drive for promotion. The loan signing from Plymouth Argyle replaced Mehew for the final 8 minutes but showed enough during that time to prove he had exciting skills and was prepared to take on defenders. Although Francis was resigned to losing Byrne at the end of his loan spell, he believed that Phil Purnell's rapid return should solve the winger gap.

With a second consecutive victory, 3 more precious points earned kept Rovers in 3rd place and in touch with the Third Division leaders proving that a haul of only 2 points from 4 league games in January was a temporary setback.

## 23 FEBRUARY 1990

|  | P | W | D | L | F | A | Pts |
|---|---|---|---|---|---|---|---|
| Bristol City | 26 | 16 | 5 | 5 | 35 | 20 | 53 |
| Tranmere Rovers | 30 | 15 | 6 | 9 | 57 | 34 | 51 |
| Notts County | 28 | 14 | 8 | 6 | 41 | 31 | 50 |
| BRISTOL ROVERS | 27 | 13 | 10 | 4 | 36 | 20 | 49 |
| Huddersfield Town | 27 | 13 | 9 | 5 | 38 | 30 | 48 |
| Rotherham United | 29 | 13 | 8 | 8 | 54 | 35 | 47 |
| Bolton Wanderers | 27 | 12 | 10 | 5 | 41 | 29 | 46 |

## Saturday 24 February 1990, Vetch Field, Swansea

Swansea City 0
Bristol Rovers 0
Half-time: 0–0
Attendance: 5,664
Referee: Kevin Breen (Liverpool)
**Swansea City:** Bracey, Hough, Coleman, Melville, Boyle, Thornber, Harris, Davey, Chalmers, Raynor, Hutchison. Substitutes: Curtis for Boyle (74 mins), Hughes (not used).
**Bristol Rovers:** Parkin, Alexander, Twentyman, Yates, Mehew, Jones, Holloway, Reece, White, Saunders, Purnell. Substitutes: Sealy (not used), Willmott (not used).

Rovers were unchanged for the fourth successive game and undefeated since the arrival of David Byrne and Carl Saunders. Byrne, whose loan period was due to finish after the Leyland Daf Southern semi-final against Walsall, was in considerable pain from a thigh strain and was considered doubtful. Striker Paul Nixon was also out of the squad with a back injury. Rovers had a fine record against Swansea, their last defeat at the Vetch was almost five years previously. The Swans had only won once in their last 6 matches but manager Ian Evans was pleased with his mid-table side's recent performances.

Three minutes into the game Carl Saunders was clumsily upended by defender Terry Boyle, but Ian Holloway's rather tame spot-kick driven low was saved by Bracey, who dived the right way. It appeared that the unfortunate penalty-taker slipped as he prepared to strike the ball.

From a 25th-minute Tommy Hutchison corner the ball skidded off Geoff Twentyman's head and Holloway made a vital goal-line clearance from Mark Harris' header, making amends for his earlier penalty failure. Swansea goalkeeper Lee Bracey – who shot to national prominence with an almost single-handed defiance of Liverpool in the FA Cup in January – made two exceptional saves, the first from Phil Purnell in the 29th minute. Carl Saunders broke down the right, zigzagged past two defenders, cut inside and swept the ball forward to Purnell who hit a rasping right-foot shot on the turn, which was instinctively blocked by Bracey. Four minutes

All eyes are on the ball as Ian Holloway has his penalty-kick saved by Swansea goalkeeper Lee Bracey at Vetch Field.

later the goalkeeper denied Ian Alexander, who was again set up by Mehew and Saunders, turning his shot around the post for a corner. The Swans gradually forced their way into the game after the interval and both Andy Reece and Vaughan Jones made vital clearances under pressure. While Saunders and Devon White continued to look dangerous up front they were receiving less of the ball as Purnell and Mehew were pinned down on the flanks. In the 75th minute Rovers threatened to break the

Steve Yates takes the ball away as Swansea defender Andrew Melville slides in to tackle him.

deadlock when in one of the best moves of the match Saunders held off several challenges before passing to Alexander whose teasing cross was cleared for a corner. Swansea's best spell came in the last quarter of an hour when Alan Curtis replaced defender Boyle and almost immediately tested Parkin with a long-range shot. Chris Coleman and Simon Davey did likewise but at no time did the Rovers defence look vulnerable as they recorded their 18th clean sheet of the season.

With only 8 minutes left Holloway broke through on the left running on to Andy Reece's through ball, but lifted his shot over the bar with only goalkeeper Bracey to beat, and 3 minutes later Rovers might have clinched the game as following another penetrating run by Alexander, Harris miskicked his clearance but White just failed to make contact with the loose ball.

The swirling wind ruined the game as a spectacle, but Rovers performed in the determined style that had earned them the best defensive record in the country, although an opportunity to reinforce their promotion challenge was lost.

## Saturday 3 March 1990, Twerton Park

**Bristol Rovers** 6 – Saunders 3, Mehew, Alexander, Holloway
**Wigan Athletic** 1 – Carberry
**Half-time**: 2–0
**Attendance**: 5,169
**Referee**: John Martin (Alton)
**Bristol Rovers**: Parkin, Alexander, Twentyman, Yates, Mehew, Jones, Holloway, Reece, White, Saunders, Purnell. Substitutes: Sealy for Saunders (82 mins), Willmott for Purnell (80 mins).
**Wigan Athletic**: Hughes, Senior, Tankard, Parkinson, Atherton, Johnson, Thompson, Rogerson, Pilling, Daley, Griffiths. Substitutes: Carberry for Rogerson (51 mins), Patterson for Griffiths (72 mins).

Carl Saunders turns to score Rovers' second goal, and his first, after 9 minutes past Wigan goalkeeper Phil Hughes.

Gerry Francis was frustrated at another postponement – the Leyland Daf Southern semi-final against Walsall scheduled for Wednesday 28 February – because if Rovers progressed in the competition there was a distinct possibility of his team having to play 3 games a week towards the end of the season. But the manager was heartened that Geoff Twentyman, after many months on the transfer list, had resolved his differences with the club, signing a new contract on the Friday before the game keeping him at Rovers until the end of the 1992 season. Rovers, in 4th position, just 3 points behind pacesetters Bristol City and Notts County, were the only team in the top five playing at home, against a Wigan side who had lost only one of their last dozen league matches and had risen from a bottom-four spot to a respectable 14th place, though their only away success had been surprisingly at Rotherham. Rovers were unchanged for the fifth successive game, with the only doubt surrounding the naming of the substitutes with Tony Sealy, Ian Willmott, Pete Cawley and Ian Hazel all vying for a place on the bench. Loan signing David Byrne had returned to Plymouth but Rovers intended watching with interest how his career developed with new Argyle manager David Kemp.

Within 3 minutes of the start of the game Rovers took the lead when Vaughan Jones put a long shot against the angle of post and crossbar and David Mehew, showing typical anticipation, nipped in to score his thirteenth goal of the season. Six minutes later the home side had doubled their lead. White soared to reach a searching free-kick delivered by Jones from way out on the left and as he headed it down his striking partner in the six-yard box swivelled and swept the ball into the goal for Saunders' fourth goal since his arrival from Stoke.

Saunders and Andy Reece then staged a quick one-two to creatively slice the Wigan defence open, but it ended with Reece's shot hitting an upright, and Mehew the crossbar, as Rovers turned on one of their best displays of the three-year Francis reign. Ian Alexander immediately stamped out Wigan's threat from the second half restart and within 12 seconds passed to Mehew to slide a pass through the middle into the path of Saunders. In four strides he was between two markers and clear for a shot at goal which he hit powerfully into the net from

Rovers go 4–1 up against Wigan as Carl Saunders completes his hat-trick with a 75th minute header.

20 yards with a magnificent drive. Casual play by Mehew, Alexander and then Twentyman allowed substitute Jim Carberry, on for the injured Lee Rogerson, to beat Brian Parkin with a low drive to score in the 72nd minute to give Wigan momentary hope. However, three minutes later Saunders notched his third goal to quickly re-establish Rovers' superiority. Twentyman rose at the far post to head another Jones free-kick across the goal and Saunders forced the ball home.

Twentyman's headed pass then set up Ian Alexander, who stormed down the right to drive in the fifth goal in the 77th minute as the Wigan defence backed off. Saunders then departed with a calf strain, but his replacement, Tony Sealy, crafted the sixth goal for Ian Holloway. With his back to goal Sealy spotted the industrious midfielder on a run and his pass invited the angled drive which beat goalkeeper Phil Hughes once more.

It now looked as though the malaise that Rovers suffered of not turning superiority into goals during a barren January which had cost them the Third Division leadership was now over, with Gerry Francis describing the team's performance as one of the best since he had been at the club. With Bob Taylor scoring a hat-trick in Bristol City's 3–0 win over Chester City a piece of Bristol football history was created, with the Robins striker and Saunders being the first players to score Football League hat-tricks for City and Rovers on the same day.

### Tuesday 6 March 1990, Elm Park, Reading

**Reading** 0
**Bristol Rovers** 1 – Mehew
**Half-time**: 0–1
**Attendance**: 6,147
**Referee**: John Moules (Erith)
**Reading**: Francis, Knight, Richardson, Wood, Hicks, Conroy, Gooding, Tait, Leworthy, Gilkes, Moran. Substitutes: Beavon for Leworthy (65 mins), Payne for Moran (65 mins).
**Bristol Rovers**: Parkin, Alexander, Twentyman, Yates, Mehew, Jones, Holloway, Reece, White, Saunders, Purnell. Substitutes: Sealy (not used), Willmott (not used).

David Mehew heads the ball past Reading goalkeeper Steve Francis for the only goal of the game at Elm Park.

Rovers travelled to Elm Park for the fifth meeting of the season between the clubs seeking their first win over Reading in eleven encounters. Reading had won six and drawn four of the 10 matches since Rovers achieved a 1–0 win at Eastville in September 1984. Reading had also been the only team to triumph at Twerton Park this season when Trevor Senior's goal settled the FA Cup second round second replay. Carl Saunders was declared fit after a slight scare over a bruised thigh suffered as he was scoring a hat-trick against Wigan, enabling Gerry Francis to name an unchanged side for the sixth match in a row. The Royals, who had only lost twice at home, were without top goalscorer Senior, sidelined after a minor throat operation following a clash with Bristol City's Robbie Turner the previous Saturday.

Saunders was denied by accomplished goalkeeper Steve Francis in the opening minute from a first-time half-volley, then Reading's only real chance, after 16 minutes, was foiled by Brian Parkin after Micky Tait had unleashed a snap shot from 12 yards and Rovers' goalkeeper leapt to his left to hold the ball. The visitors should have taken the lead in the 20th minute when Devon White contrived to head over an open goal from Vaughan Jones' curling cross which had just eluded Saunders' head, and David Mehew should have done better from 8 yards after Saunders slipped his marker and created an opening, but Mehew's attempted lay-off to Vaughan Jones went wide of him. After 30 minutes Rovers went ahead when Ian Holloway lifted a right-footed inswinger from the left just short of the near post, Devon White made the deflection and Mehew glanced in a header past Francis for his 14th goal of the season.

The home side's defence was frequently exposed, particularly down the left where Jones and Purnell flourished, and one Jones cross almost found Saunders in the 38th minute but was plucked from his head by the tips of Steve Francis' outstretched fingers. Rovers continued to attack after the break with Reece twice blasting wide, and Phil Purnell spurned the chance of an obvious penalty in the 61st-minute after Steve Richardson took a flying lunge at the winger in the penalty area. Instead of falling, Purnell stayed on his feet, kept going to fire a shot at the advancing Francis, who deprived 'Percy' of his first goal of the season. Geoff Twentyman volleyed against the bar from a corner, and Reading manager Ian Porterfield brought on a double substitution in attack in a last-ditch attempt to salvage the

David Mehew side-foots the ball into the Reading net, but his effort was disallowed because of a Devon White foul on defender Martin Hicks.

game, but Rovers looked too solid to buckle, and continued to press forward. With 2 minutes remaining Holloway again swung over a flag-kick and the well-practised corner routine again found White's head for Mehew to 'score', but the goal was disallowed as Rovers' big striker was adjudged to have elbowed defender Martin Hicks to the ground.

Corner and free-kick routines were testimony to the coaching of manager Gerry Francis, but the side's other trademarks – effort, selfless teamwork and swift, incisive counter-attacking from the back, harnessed to a high degree – were always evident as Rovers buried their Reading jinx, and moved into 2nd place in the league above their local rivals when City were beaten 3–1 at Ashton Gate by Tranmere Rovers, who took over the top spot.

### Sunday 11 March 1990, Twerton Park

**Bristol Rovers** 0
**Leyton Orient** 0
**Half-time**: 0–0
**Attendance**: 7,018
**Referee**: Edward Parker (Preston)
**Bristol Rovers**: Parkin, Alexander, Twentyman, Yates, Mehew, Jones, Holloway, Reece, White, Saunders, Purnell. Substitutes: Sealy (not used), Willmott (not used).
**Leyton Orient**: Heald, Hales, Dickenson, Beesley, Day, Sitton, Howard, Hoddle, Sayer, Cooper, Baker. Substitutes: Fashanu for Sayer (63 mins), Baker (not used).

As both Bath City and Rovers had been given home fixtures at Twerton Park on Saturday 10 March, Rovers switched the league match to the following day, their third Sunday home game of the season. Rovers fielded the same side that had ended Reading's recent domination over the Pirates, whilst former Newcastle United and Nottingham Forest stalwart Frank Clark's East London side included a number of familiar players, including former Chelsea defenders John Sitton and Kevin Hales, Carl Hoddle, younger brother of England international Glenn, and Justin Fashanu, Britain's first £1m black footballer.

Rovers, in front of Twerton Park's second-best league crowd of the season, did little to impress them from their display in the opening 45 minutes, defending soundly but moving forward with little purpose or cohesion, although the home side let Orient off the hook 2 minutes from half-time. Phil Purnell crossed from the left, Devon White dummied and David

Carl Saunders, Geoff Twentyman and Devon White appeal for a penalty during the Leyton Orient match, but referee Edward Parker remained unconvinced.

Mehew was left with the type of close-range chance he normally put away with aplomb. But he tried to place the ball past Paul Heald, hit it tamely and the young goalkeeper saved. There was a big improvement after the break, Mehew roamed from flank to flank and made more positive runs and Andy Reece upped his game to give the industrious Holloway better support in the centre of midfield. Purnell missed another great opportunity to put the Pirates in front 7 minutes into the second half when Carl Saunders, who again impressed with his pace and skills, broke down the right and squared a perfect low pass. This gave the unmarked Purnell with an easy opportunity to score, but he sent his shot back across the goal and wide.

One brief moment of concern for Rovers followed the arrival of Justin Fashanu as Orient's substitute. Ian Holloway cleared off the line from the former Norwich and Nottingham Forest striker following a corner which was disputed by Brian Parkin, leading to Rovers' goalkeeper being booked. Mehew's shot was brilliantly turned around the post by Heald and from Reece's resulting corner, Geoff Twentyman headed against the top of the far post. Devon White's header from another Reece corner was cleared off Orient's goal line by Kevin Dickenson, and then Saunders' carving a chance out of nothing, slipped the ball inches wide of the far post with a shot from the left. And there were strong claims for penalties when White and later Mehew were bundled over off the ball when close to goal, but referee Edward Parker would have none of it and waved play on.

Orient manager Frank Clark offered encouragement to Rovers supporters worried about two more dropped home points, as in his view Rovers were promotion bound, stating that, 'No side has put us under greater pressure away from home this season and Gerry Francis must be very disappointed not to have won the game', as indeed he was. 'We played well enough to have won the game easily but dropped points through a combination of missed chances, bad luck and some poor refereeing decisions,' said Rovers' manager, whose side had to be content with seven draws in their sixteen-match unbeaten home league run.

## Wednesday 14 March 1990, Twerton Park
## Leyland Daf Cup Southern Semi-Final

Bristol Rovers 0
Walsall 0
Half-time: 0–0
Bristol Rovers won 3–2 on penalties after extra time. Rovers' scorers: Holloway, Jones, Reece. Walsall scorers: Skipper, Mower
Attendance: 4,740
**Referee**: Roger Gifford (Llanbardach)
**Bristol Rovers**: Parkin, Alexander, Twentyman, Yates, Mehew, Jones, Holloway, Reece, White, Saunders, Purnell. Substitutes: Sealy for Mehew (113 mins), Willmott (not used).
**Walsall**: Barber, Rees, Mower, Taylor, Forbes, Skipper, Goodwin, Rimmer, Bertschin, Hawker, Littlejohn. Substitutes: Hart for Bertschin (120 mins), Kelly (not used).

With Walsall looking relegation certainties for the second time in two years, manager John Barnwell was banking on a Wembley appearance to salvage his season and keep him his job. Kenny Hibbitt, who played under Barnwell at Wolves, was hoping the Saddlers lost the Cup tie but managed to stay in the Third Division, with Rovers hoping to complete a hat-trick of wins having already beaten Walsall 2–1 at Fellows Park and 2–0 at home.

After just 3 minutes, leading scorer David Mehew forced goalkeeper Fred Barber into a near-post save after Phil Purnell had crossed from the left. Andy Reece became an early entry in referee Roger Gifford's notebook in the 10th minute for a late challenge on Mark Goodwin and 2 minutes later Purnell and Stuart Rimmer followed him into the book – and could count themselves lucky not to have been sent off. Both players ended up trading punches after Rimmer had brought down Rovers' winger and had to be separated by their teammates. Walsall were determined not to see a repeat of the previous month's 2–0 league defeat and put up a brave defence marshalled by the aptly named captain Peter Skipper. It wasn't until the 26th minute that Rovers seriously threatened Walsall's goal when Devon White's header was cleared by defender Graeme Forbes. Andy Reece then had two chances in the final 5 minutes of the first half; a powerful left-footed drive from 25 yards in the 40th minute crashed against the crossbar before Barber tipped a looping header over the top on the stroke of half-time.

Captian Vaughan Jones hammers penalty number two past Walsall goalkeeper Fred Barber in the Leyland Daf Cup penalty shoot-out.

Brian Parkin saves Walsall's fifth penalty, taken by Stuart Rimmer, to secure victory in the Southern Area semi-final.

The pace of the game quickened after the interval and Peter Skipper had a 49th-minute 20-yard drive cleared off the goal line by Vaughan Jones. Carl Saunders was given little room for manoeuvre by the resolute Walsall defence but managed to deceive marker Graeme Forbes to attempt a volley on the turn in the 72nd minute. Seconds later David Mehew had the best chance to put Rovers ahead, but he appeared too casual in trying to place Alexander's long through ball past goalkeeper Barber. Brian Parkin saw little of the ball until the latter stages of the match but twice produced vital saves when Rimmer broke through – the most crucial after 68 minutes when put clean through by Littlejohn – and after two hours of goalless action the match was decided on penalty kicks.

Parkin saved Walsall's first penalty, Mark Rees' effort, with a low dive to his right, before Ian Holloway put Rovers ahead. Peter Skipper equalised only for Vaughan Jones to re-establish Rovers' advantage. Kenny Mower levelled the scores before Phil Purnell had his tame shot saved by Barber. Then Walsall substitute Peter Hart's penalty was stopped by Parkin before Andy Reece netted. Stuart Rimmer, Walsall's leading marksman in three consecutive seasons, then had the Saddlers final penalty kick saved by Brian Parkin diving to his left, so Geoff Twentyman – who converted the decisive penalty at Brentford – was not required.

Parkin dashed to the crowd in jubilation – and was carried aloft across the field by fans to the dressing rooms at the end of a nail-biting finale – after his superb goalkeeping display sent Gerry Francis' team into the Southern Area two-leg final with Notts County and kept Rovers' hopes of a first Wembley final alive.

## Saturday 17 March 1990, Craven Cottage, Fulham

**Fulham** 1 – Walker
**Bristol Rovers** 2 – White 2
**Half-time**: 0–0
**Attendance**: 5,656
**Referee**: Jim Borrett (Harleston)
**Fulham**: Batty, Newson, Pike, Mauge, Nebbling, Eckhardt, Davies, Scott, Milton, Marshall, Walker. Substitutes: Barnett for Marshall (72 mins), Bremner (not used).
**Bristol Rovers**: Parkin, Alexander, Twentyman, Yates, Mehew, Jones, Holloway, Reece, White, Saunders, Purnell. Substitutes: Sealy for Mehew (75 mins), Willmott (not used).

Only one goal in the previous 3 games was hardly the stuff of promotion candidates but Gerry Francis was not unduly concerned, stating that, 'The time to worry is when you are not creating any chances.' But Rovers needed to rediscover their scoring touch, as excluding the recent 6–1 hammering of Wigan, they had scored only seven times in the previous 9 league games. However, defensively Rovers boasted the best record in the Football league with only four defeats – equal with Liverpool and Sheffield United – and just 21 goals conceded in 31 games. Rovers' most recent visit to Craven Cottage was the 4–0 victory in the previous season's play-off semi-final, but Fulham, their defence strengthened since the £125,000 signing of Mark Newson from Bournemouth ,were on a run of three straight wins.

Fulham's new captain denied Rovers an opening goal after 20 minutes, when home goalkeeper Lawrence Batty missed a Mehew cross and Carl Saunders' shot hit Jeff Eckhardt and sped towards the goal line only for Newson, facing his own goal, to scramble it to safety. Rovers had a double let-off 10 minutes later, when former Welsh international Gordon Davies sent a glancing header crashing against a post from Clive Walker's cross, and seconds later Davies found Steve Milton in the Rovers area and the striker turned to shoot, but only into the side netting. Walker was booked for handball after disputing a Rovers free-kick, but Ronnie Mauge escaped with a warning after going in late on Brian Parkin. After 58 minutes Newson became the second Fulham player to be cautioned. In the 63rd minute Rovers took the lead when

Devon White hits a volley from Ian Holloway's pass to score Rovers' winning goal at Fulham.

Saunders, who had caused problems for Fulham's John Marshall all afternoon, got free down the left and crossed to the far post for the unmarked Devon White to side-foot home with a volley for his seventh goal of the season.

For a while Fulham looked dangerous after their 74th-minute equaliser brought them back into the game. Clive Walker's mishit shot from the edge of a packed penalty area hit Steve Yates, before taking another deflection off Vaughan Jones and rolled into the net off the post. Brian Parkin then made two outstanding leaps to his left to keep out shots from Walker and then Pike. With 7 minutes left and both teams appearing content with a draw Devon White met Ian Holloway's cross to secure all 3 points for the Pirates. Ian Alexander pumped the ball down the right to Holloway where the industrious midfielder took the ball to the byline. The Fulham fans looked for the referee to award their side a goal-kick, thinking that the ball had gone over the line, but Holloway carried on at the referee's insistence, squared the ball back to White who rocketed it in from 10 yards, almost taking the 'keeper's head off in the process. With a minute remaining White had the chance to end the match with a hat-trick but his header from Holloway's cross lacked power.

Devon White's 2 second-half goals ended his 19-game barren spell stretching back to the beginning of December and set up a Rovers victory that added fresh impetus to their promotion challenge, extending their unbeaten run to 11 games. The 3 points were an encouraging prelude to a hectic eighteen days with Rovers scheduled to play six times, and with manager Francis only having a pool of seventeen players available he prepared to go into the marketplace for two or three more players to strengthen the side in the coming weeks.

## 17 MARCH 1990

|                   | P  | W  | D  | L  | F  | A  | Pts |
|-------------------|----|----|----|----|----|----|-----|
| Tranmere Rovers   | 35 | 20 | 6  | 9  | 69 | 35 | 66  |
| Bristol City      | 32 | 20 | 5  | 7  | 45 | 25 | 65  |
| BRISTOL ROVERS    | 32 | 16 | 12 | 4  | 45 | 22 | 60  |
| Notts County      | 34 | 17 | 8  | 9  | 48 | 40 | 59  |
| Bolton Wanderers  | 32 | 15 | 10 | 7  | 48 | 34 | 55  |
| Bury              | 35 | 15 | 8  | 12 | 51 | 42 | 53  |
| Rotherham United  | 34 | 14 | 9  | 11 | 59 | 46 | 51  |

## Wednesday 21 March 1990, Twerton Park

**Bristol Rovers** 2 – White, Purnell
**Bury** 1 – Hoyland
**Half-time**: 0–1
**Attendance**: 5,552
**Referee**: Danny Vickers (Ilford)
**Bristol Rovers**: Parkin, Alexander, Twentyman, Yates, Mehew, Jones, Holloway, Reece, White, Saunders, Purnell. Substitutes: Sealy for Saunders (68 mins), Willmott (not used).
**Bury**: Kelly, Hill, Bishop, Valentine, Knill, Lee, Patterson, Hoyland, Parkinson, Robinson, Hulme. Substitutes: Feeley (not used), Withe (not used).

Third placed Rovers, needing a home victory to keep up their challenge for an automatic promotion spot, had Geoff Twentyman (ankle injury) and Phil Purnell (knee) under intense treatment on Tuesday, but both were likely to feature in an unchanged side. Brian Parkin also missed training with a slight knock. Bury, who had won their last 4 games, arrived at Twerton with one of the best away records in Division Three, the Shakers specialising in big results at the least likely of venues; 4–1 at Notts County and 4–2 at Tranmere Rovers.

In only the 7th minute, midfield player Mark Patterson intercepted Steve Yates' backpass and struck the ball narrowly wide after beating Brian Parkin, and then Jamie Hoyland's 23rd-minute goal provided some pattern to a frenetic start and gave the visitors a well-deserved lead. Patterson found David Lee on the right and he held off Vaughan Jones' challenge to cross for Hoyland to glance in a neat header from just inside the penalty area, with Rovers' defenders motionless. Within a minute Devon White headed just off target from an Ian Holloway corner and then Bury goalkeeper Gary Kelly was caught out trying to fist away outside his eighteen-yard box as Carl Saunders closed in. From the resulting free-kick, Jones' shot came off the defensive wall for a corner. Phil Purnell's left-wing runs were promising for Rovers and from one such raid just before the interval he set up Geoff Twentyman,

David Mehew has a powerful drive charged down by Bury goalkeeper Gary Kelly.

but the defender's shot flew past Kelly's left-hand post. Twentyman could have done better with another chance a minute later as Saunders nodded on a Holloway cross.

Rovers emerged from the break with reformed character, following a Gerry Francis half-time tactical change that provided more cover from midfield for his full-backs, but Devon White missed a free header and then shot straight at the Bury goalkeeper after 69 minutes. However, he redeemed himself a minute later when he swung himself at David Mehew's deep cross and the ball flew in the net off the striker's thigh over the despairing Gary Kelly. Fortunes were transformed and Bury had no answer to their opponents' renewed commitment. Phil Purnell, darting into the penalty area, headed in a Vaughan Jones long-throw 7 minutes from time to complete Rovers' recovery. It was the winger's first goal for more than a year, much of which had been spent recovering from a knee injury.

For a long period Bury looked like inflicting an embarrassing defeat on an out-of-sorts Rovers who struggled to put passes together, but it was a never-say-die performance by the home side when they eventually realised the need to inject greater urgency, pace and purpose to ultimately outplay Bury at their own game. The win increased Rovers' unbeaten run and left the Pirates 3 points behind second-placed Tranmere with 2 games in hand on the Birkenhead club.

## Saturday 24 March 1990, Twerton Park

**Bristol Rovers** 2 – Nixon, Mehew
**Cardiff City** 1 – Rodgerson
**Half-time**: 0–1
**Attendance**: 4,631
**Referee**: Ray Bigger (Croydon)
**Bristol Rovers**: Parkin, Alexander, Twentyman, Yates, Mehew, Jones, Holloway, Reece, White, Sealy, Purnell. Substitutes: Nixon for Sealy (half-time), Willmott (not used).
**Cardiff City**: Hansbury, Rodgerson, Blake, Barnard, Abraham, Gibbins, Morgan, Griffith, Pike, Perry, Chandler. Substitutes: Scott for Chandler (89 mins), Gummer (not used).

Because of recent problems with Cardiff City supporters the Welsh FA had put restrictions in place on Bluebirds fans travelling to away matches. For the all-ticket Severnside derby, Cardiff only sold tickets to season ticket holders and members of the supporters' club and the kick-off time was move forward to midday. Rovers needed a win or a draw to equal their record home run of 27 games without defeat and to add spice to the encounter, was the knowledge that Cardiff were the last side to take 3 points at Twerton – on 4 February 1989. Gerry Francis entered the transfer market and secured two new players shortly before the transfer deadline on Thursday afternoon, signing versatile utility player Bob Bloomer from Chesterfield for £20,000 and Hull City goalkeeper Gavin Kelly on loan. Rovers' boss commented that the signings were vital to his team maintaining their challenge at the top, particularly as Vaughan Jones, Christian McClean, Phil Purnell, Ian Hazel and Carl Saunders were being treated for injuries and with the threat of losing Devon White through suspension.

Playing into a strong wind and weighting their passes badly, Rovers were stunned when Cardiff took the lead in the 14th minute, in front of a disappointingly small attendance, having missed two early opportunities from Sealy and Reece. The visitors won a free-kick when Ian Alexander obligingly back-heeled the ball to Chris Pike who was then knocked over by Geoff Twentyman on the edge of Rovers' penalty area. The set-piece had been well rehearsed. Morgan set up a dummy, Leigh Barnard rolled the ball invitingly in front of Ian Rodgerson – the only survivor from Cardiff's team from the last shock meeting in Bath – and the full-back unleashed a 20-yard drive that beat goalkeeper Brian Parkin's dive. Len Ashurst's side then fell back on their tried and trusted sweeper system in an effort to hold on to what they had. In the 22nd minute, Devon White felled goalkeeper Hansbury as they both jumped for the ball, and it was a full 4 minutes before he got to his feet again.

Paul Nixon scores Rovers' 88th-minute equaliser with Cardiff goalkeeper Roger Hansbury grounded.

David Mehew rises above a crowd of Cardiff defenders to head an injury-time winner in the Severnside derby.

Paul Nixon, taken off the transfer list following discussions with Gerry Francis, came on after half-time as substitute for the injured Tony Sealy – a replacement for the unfit Carl Saunders – who was taken to hospital for a X-ray on his right ankle. It was the New Zealand international's first senior game for nearly two months. After the interval, Rovers' pressure increased and Phil Purnell shot over the bar from 5 yards.

With time running out Rovers maintained their pressure on the besieged Cardiff defence and were rewarded with an equaliser in the 88th minute in controversial circumstances. Cardiff goalkeeper Hansbury was allegedly bundled off the ball as home striker Devon White rose to meet Vaughan Jones' long throw-in. As the players crashed to the ground, Paul Nixon forced the ball over the line, as Hansbury's teammates vehemently claimed a free-kick should have been awarded for a foul on the goalkeeper. Rovers then threw everything at the Cardiff goal in search of maximum points and 4 minutes into injury time Phil Purnell turned the ball in from the edge of the penalty area and David Mehew found the top corner of the net with a header on the run, for his fifteenth goal of the season. Referee Ray Bigger, in his first season on the Football League list, needed a police escort to leave the pitch as Cardiff manager Len Ashurst tried to calm his enraged players.

Both goalscorer Paul Nixon and Gerry Francis admitted afterwards that they wouldn't have been surprised if a free-kick had been awarded instead of the equalising goal, but Rovers' late 'Houdini Act' that won 3 priceless points strengthened their promotion challenge, as rivals Notts County and Bristol City played out a goalless draw and Tranmere Rovers were defeated at Mansfield.

## Wednesday 28 March 1990, Twerton Park
## Leyland Daf Cup Southern Area Final, first leg

**Bristol Rovers** 1 – Mehew
**Notts County** 0
**Half-time**: 0–0
**Attendance**: 6,480
**Referee**: Alan Seville (Birmingham)
**Bristol Rovers**: Parkin, Alexander, Twentyman, Yates, Mehew, Jones, Holloway, Reece, White, Nixon, Purnell. Substitutes: McClean for Reece (76 mins), Willmott (not used).
**Notts County**: Cherry, O'Riordan, Platnauer, Short, Yates, Robinson, Norton, Turner, Chapman, Bartlett, Johnson. Substitutes: Stant for Bartlett (83 mins), Law (not used).

Rival promotion candidates Notts County like Rovers had reached the Southern Area Final of the Leyland Daf competition for the first time, after overcoming Fulham and Peterborough United in the early stages, before single goal victories at Bristol City, Hereford United and Maidstone United. Gerry Francis expected Neil Warnock's side to aim for a draw, considering that the Magpies would be happy to take Rovers back to Meadow Lane with a goalless scoresheet. 'Two-leg matches are completely different affairs to a one-off situation', he said. The Rovers boss, hoping to build a convincing lead in the first leg, selected the side that finished Saturday's win over Cardiff City, with Paul Nixon partnering Devon White up front; new signing Bob Bloomer was cup-tied for the competition. County right-back Charlie Palmer missed the game with a knee ligament injury.

Notts County made by far the better start on a dry mild evening, threatening with several darting runs from strikers Gary Chapman and Kevin Bartlett, a recent signing from West Bromwich Albion. After only 6 minutes goalkeeper Brian Parkin was forced to pull off a superb fingertip save to deny Craig Short's free header from Tommy Johnson's cross. And it was Parkin again who came to the rescue in the 21st minute when he raced to the edge of the area to save bravely at the feet of the lively Bartlett. After being placed under the hammer for much of the first half, by a Notts County team looking nothing like a side

From Devon White's flick-on, David Mehew heads past Notts County's Steve Cherry to score the only goal of the Leyland Daf Area Final at Twerton Park.

content to settle for an away draw, Rovers became more direct and purposeful after the half-time break. Paul Nixon, impressively partnering Devon White up front in the absence of Carl Saunders and Tony Sealy, hit a half-volley narrowly over the crossbar in the 53rd minute, and 10 minutes later Andy Reece drove inches wide of the far post from 25 yards, while Phil Purnell might have done better with an effort shortly afterwards. Ian Alexander, enjoying a fine game at right-back, broke down the flank and his cross was flicked on by Devon White to Purnell but he shot over the crossbar from the edge of the penalty area. Gerry Francis replaced Andy Reece with Christian McClean in the 76th minute and made a tactical switch, moving David Mehew to a central role, the subtle move unlocking the tense midfield battle 2 minutes later. Mehew put Devon White away but his shot was deflected round a post by goalkeeper Cherry. From the resulting Holloway corner McClean moved into the box, allowing White to flick-on the ball with his head for Mehew to head past Cherry from close-range to the delight of the Twerton faithful.

Paul Nixon went close in the final minute with a terrific 25-yard shot, which had it gone in would have significantly increased Rovers' chance of appearing in a Wembley final. After the match, however, County manager Neil Warnock warned Rovers, 'Don't book your Wembley tickets yet. We have a good home record and our supporters will give us tremendous encouragement. Having got this far, our players are determined to go all the way.' Gerry Francis was reasonably pleased with the result but unhappy with his side's performance. 'I felt that some of the players froze and allowed the occasion to get to them, and we didn't play well in the first half. Notts County will make a very tough game of it next week, but we have given ourselves a good fighting chance,' he said.

## Saturday 31 March 1990, County Ground, Northampton

**Northampton Town** 1 – Thorpe
**Bristol Rovers** 2 – McClean, Holloway
**Half-time**: 0–0
**Attendance**: 3,774
**Referee**: William Flood (Stockport)
**Northampton Town**: Gleasure, Chard, Wilson, Terry, Wilcox, Donald, Berry, Collins, Leaburn, Barnes, Thorpe. Substitutes: Sandeman for Chard (60 mins), Brown (not used).
**Bristol Rovers**: Parkin, Alexander, Twentyman, Yates, Mehew, Jones, Holloway, Reece, McClean, Nixon, Purnell. Substitutes: Willmott for Alexander (49 mins), Saunders for Nixon (58 mins).

The *Bristol Evening Post* on the day of the match suggested that Rovers needed to aim for at least 87 points to gain automatic promotion to the Second Division, providing statistics compiled over the previous eight seasons that revealed that the average points tally for Third Division runners-up was 86.5. Prior to the game at the County Ground, Rovers required twenty-one points to reach the target from 12 remaining games. The average number of points required to win the Third Division championship over the previous eight seasons was 92. Devon White started his third suspension of the season. Having served bans already for a sending-off at Chester in October and for reaching 21 disciplinary points in January, he had now exceeded the 30-point limit. Carl Saunders recovered from his hamstring strain was included in the squad, but Tony Sealy was ruled out after two sets of X-rays had failed to show what was wrong with his leg. Northampton, with only Walsall below them in the league table, were seeking their first win for 14 games.

Bobby Barnes' speed and skill had Rovers' defence in all sorts of trouble early on and goalkeeper Brian Parkin needed to be alert to deny the Cobblers a first half lead. Paul Nixon

Christian McClean reacts quickly to goalkeeper Gleasure's fumble to score Rovers' equalising goal at Northampton.

Ian Holloway scores a long-range winner at Northampton. Rovers won 2–1.

had the best chance to put the visitors ahead but his close-range half-volley from Ian Holloway's 24th-minute corner was well saved by goalkeeper Peter Gleasure. In the 29th minute Holloway left the field with blood streaming down his face after a clash with Northampton's Steve Berry. Thirteen minutes and four stitches later he returned to rapturous applause from a large Rovers following. Only some desperate defending, in particular from Geoff Twentyman, kept out goal-bound efforts from both Chard and Carl Leaburn, on a month's loan from First Division Charlton Athletic, in the 34th minute.

Ian Willmott replaced the injured Ian Alexander in defence 4 minutes after the interval, before Nixon, another casualty was substituted by Carl Saunders in the 58th minute. Northampton took the lead after 62 minutes when Berry's free-kick was headed on by Leaburn and new signing Adrian Thorpe marked his home debut with a well-struck volley from 15 yards. The cheers from the home fans had hardly died down when, in the 63rd minute, Rovers were permanently reduced to ten men as Andy Reece was sent off together with Warren Donald. Reece retaliated after being on the end of a horrendous foul by the Northampton man – but the red card seemed harsh punishment.

Rovers then proceeded to dominate the action with McClean and Twentyman going close, before a low 75th-minute Saunders shot slipped under Gleasure and McClean rammed the ball into an empty net. Deputising for the suspended Devon White and playing his first full game in three months, the tall striker marked a fine display with a crucial equaliser. As the seconds ticked away, Steve Yates had a brilliant 30-yard effort well saved by Gleasure, and from the resulting corner, Phil Purnell found Ian Holloway on the edge of the penalty area, who jinked inside before unleashing an unstoppable 20-yard shot into the roof of the net beyond the flailing arms of Gleasure, to the joy of the massed Rovers fans behind the goal.

For the third league game running the Third Division promotion contenders had come from behind to win 2–1, although Gerry Francis was again disappointed with a poor first-half display but credited his players for their determined effort. 'These late wins aren't doing my health a lot of good, but we're getting there in the end,' commented Rovers' manager.

## Monday 2 April 1990. Meadow Lane, Nottingham
## Leyland Daf Cup Southern Area Final, second leg

**Notts County** 0
**Bristol Rovers** 0
**Half-time**: 0–0
**Attendance**: 10,857
**Referee**: Brian Hill (Kettering)
**Notts County**: Cherry, Norton, Platnauer, Short, Yates, Robinson, O'Riordan, Turner, Chapman, Bartlett, Johnson. Substitutes: Stant for Bartlett (67 mins), Lund for O'Riordan (76 mins).
**Bristol Rovers**: Parkin, Alexander, Twentyman, Yates, Mehew, Jones, Holloway, Reece, McClean, Saunders, Purnell. Substitutes: Nixon for Purnell (89 mins), Willmott (not used).

Captain Vaughan Jones pledged that Rovers would set out to attack in the second leg of the Southern Area Final against Notts County, discounting the notion that Gerry Francis' side would simply try and safeguard their one-goal advantage. 'To sit back on such a narrow advantage would be crazy. We are quite capable of beating any side on the day and we'll be going to Meadow Lane looking for victory,' he said. Rovers were still without White (suspended), Sealy (shin injury), and Bloomer (cup-tied), whilst under treatment for minor injuries were Alexander (ankle), McClean and Jones (both groin), Nixon (left ankle) and Reece (right hip). Thousands of Rovers fans hit the M5 hoping to witness at least a draw that would bring the Pirates a first Wembley appearance in their 107-year history. County had lost only twice at home all season, conceding just 12 goals in 18 matches. Rovers' impressive away record was about to be sternly tested.

The game began at a furious pace with Rovers showing that they did not intend to sit on their one goal lead, but with the marking tight, chances were rare and it took County until the 31st minute to force their first corner. There was little to choose between the two teams in

With a first-ever trip to Wembley assured, Rovers' players celebrate in front of their travelling fans at Meadow Lane.

the first half, although County had the best chance to level the aggregate score 5 minutes before the break. Speedy striker Gary Chapman escaped the attentions of Geoff Twentyman and from the by-line crossed for Tommy Johnson to fire a 20-yard shot against the underside of the crossbar with Parkin beaten. During the interval ground staff pointedly repainted the penalty spots, possibly anticipating another extra time shoot-out.

County, who strangely persisted with their five-man defence until the final 15 minutes, created little of note and when they broke through Brian Parkin was in fine form. Efforts rained in on Rovers' goal but the back four, inspired by the commanding Steve Yates cleared everything. Carl Saunders provided rare relief with a brilliant 62nd-minute shot on the turn which required a sharp save from goalkeeper Steve Cherry. County's large and intimidating crowd demanded a final onslaught and David Norton responded with a fine strike after 75 minutes, which required a sharp save from Parkin. The goalkeeper then surpassed that to deny Craig Short a minute later and was down well to the defender's far post header. With just one minute remaining, and Rovers under desperate pressure, County forced the ball past Parkin, but referee Brian Hill controversially disallowed substitute Phil Stant's header for pushing in the area. He was immediately besieged by County players led by former Rovers player Nicky Platnauer, who had to be dragged away by Geoff Twentyman. The Rovers defender was at the centre of the controversy over the 'goal', claiming that as the ball came over from a free-kick he was hit in the back by Falklands War veteran Stant. The referee blew immediately for the foul, before the ball was actually in the net to the relief of all Rovers supporters.

The final whistle went barely a minute after the incident and was greeted by a crescendo of noise from the massed ranks of Rovers fans, celebrating that Rovers' defence had withstood the sternest of tests. More than 2,500 faithful followers cheered wildly as Gerry Francis ran across the pitch to embrace his heroes, and amid the scenes of jubilation then led the whole team back on to the pitch 10 minutes after the end, to acclaim Rovers' first ever Wembley appearance on 20 May against either Tranmere Rovers or Doncaster Rovers.

## Wednesday 4 April 1990, Springfield Park, Wigan

**Wigan Athletic** 1 – Baraclough
**Bristol Rovers** 2 – Mehew, McClean
**Half-time**: 1–0
**Attendance**: 2,352
**Referee**: Gary Aplin (Kendal)
**Wigan Athletic**: Hughes, Senior, Atherton, Johnson, Tankard, Griffiths, Hilditch, Parkinson, Carberry, Daley, Baraclough. Substitutes: Paterson for Carberry (81 mins), Page for Daley (81 mins).
**Bristol Rovers**: Parkin, Alexander, Twentyman, Yates, Mehew, Jones, Holloway, Reece, McClean, Saunders, Purnell. Substitutes: White for Reece (57 mins), Willmott (not used).

'Winning promotion comes first' was the message from Gerry Francis to his Rovers team as he attempted to bring the players down to earth after their great achievement in getting to Wembley. 'Our objective for two seasons has been promotion and, as far as I am concerned, we can dismiss Wembley until the league season is over,' he said, as a victory over Wigan would leap-frog the Pirates over Tranmere into 2nd place behind Bristol City. Wigan, with one of the best home records in the division, losing only 3 games, were keen to avenge their disastrous performance at Twerton Park which saw them lose 6–1. Christian McClean, who played a leading role in the Leyland Daf tie at Notts County, continued to partner Carl Saunders up front despite Devon White's return from his third suspension. Saunders' 3 goals against Wigan at Twerton in March took his total to 6 in 5 games, but the striker had not found the net since.

Rovers, despite playing superior football and monopolising much of the early play, trailed to a brilliantly worked goal in the 9th minute. Jimmy Carberry set left-back Tankard away on the flank and his cross was spectacularly volleyed home from 15 yards by Ian Baraclough, the striker's first goal since arriving on loan from Leicester City. There were chances to level, but twice Mehew was disappointed when his subtle flicks were cleared off the goal line by defenders, the first a header just 3 minutes after the opening goal from one of Rovers' seven first-half corners. In the 28th minute Vaughan Jones had a low drive tipped around a post by goalkeeper Phil Hughes and from that corner Mehew was denied for the second time. As the second half progressed, there seemed doubts whether Rovers would be able to extend their unbeaten run to 17 games. Gerry Francis reorganised his side in the 57th minute, introducing Devon White for midfielder Andy Reece, to play up front with Saunders. Mehew moved to central midfield and McClean to the right flank. Carl Saunders, who had an inspired final half-hour, worked the best opening for Phil Purnell who shot across the goal in the 68th minute, and then Vaughan Jones had two free-kicks from the edge of the penalty area charged down. But the break came through Wigan's slackness and a weak clearance by goalkeeper Phil Hughes. In the 74th minute, from the goalkeeper's clearance the ball eventually reached Mehew who completed a positive run into the penalty area with a cracking left-foot shot past Hughes for his seventeenth goal of the season. Relentless attacking increased the prospect of a Rovers double and as customary in recent fixtures the decisive goal came late in the game, to test the patience of another huge gallery of travelling Bristolians who outshouted and probably outnumbered home followers. This one came in the 80th minute, inevitably from another set-piece. A Holloway corner on the right was headed on by Devon White for Christian McClean to sweep in a first-time shot from 8 yards for his third goal in 4 league appearances.

Gerry Francis paid tribute to his players' character and fitness after the club's third triumph in five days, and revealed that he gave the players tough morning workouts before the last 2 games. The victory was the fifth successive 2–1 league triumph and remarkably Rovers had been behind in each, only scoring the winner in the final few minutes. It stretched their unbeaten run to 17 matches – on a ground where they had lost in the previous five seasons – and moved them into 2nd place above Tranmere, 4 points behind leaders Bristol City with a game in hand.

## 6 APRIL 1990

|  | P | W | D | L | F | A | Pts |
|---|---|---|---|---|---|---|---|
| Bristol City | 37 | 23 | 7 | 7 | 56 | 28 | 76 |
| BRISTOL ROVERS | 36 | 20 | 12 | 4 | 53 | 26 | 72 |
| Tranmere Rovers | 38 | 21 | 7 | 10 | 74 | 38 | 70 |
| Notts County | 36 | 18 | 9 | 9 | 52 | 42 | 63 |
| Bolton Wanderers | 37 | 16 | 12 | 9 | 51 | 37 | 60 |
| Bury | 38 | 16 | 9 | 13 | 53 | 44 | 57 |
| Rotherham United | 38 | 15 | 10 | 13 | 64 | 53 | 55 |

## Saturday 7 April 1990, Twerton Park

**Bristol Rovers** 2 – Mehew, McClean
**Chester City** 1 – Reeves
**Half-time**: 2–1
**Attendance**: 6,589
**Referee**: Gurnam Singh (Wolverhampton)
**Bristol Rovers**: Parkin, Alexander, Twentyman, Yates, Mehew, Jones, Holloway, Reece, McClean, Saunders, Purnell. Substitutes: White for Reece (65 mins), Willmott (not used).
**Chester City**: Stewart, Reeves, Lane, Abel, Lightfoot, Woodthorpe, Butler, Barrow, Croft, Dale, Bennett. Substitutes: Painter for Bennett (85 mins), Wynne (not used).

David Mehew knocks in his eighteenth goal of the season after just 10 minutes against Chester City.

Christian McClean had waited patiently for his chance having only played 5 league and cup games all season until called up for game at Northampton, and had responded with 2 goals in 3 games. As a result Rovers' manager kept Devon White on the substitutes' bench and might well have been reluctant to play him against Chester anyway as the striker had been sent off twice in their last three meetings, including the goalless draw earlier in the season. Chester came to Twerton boasting a single win in 19 away games and a mere 8 goals scored.

Ian Holloway set up Rovers' first goal in the 10th minute when he made a diagonal run to the right before switching his cross back over a crowded Chester defence. Two defenders missed the ball as they jumped with McClean and it fell for the unmarked David Mehew to drive in his season's eighteenth goal.

Fourteen minutes later Rovers were two up as Christian McClean bravely thrust himself between Chester's central defenders for his third goal in 4 first-team appearances – but it was a goal he knew nothing about. The striker was knocked out when Graham Abel accidently struck him on the side of the jaw as he got the important touch to Vaughan Jones' left-wing centre to loop his header over Billy Stewart and beat defender Colin Woodthorpe's attempt to clear off the line. Physio' Roy Dolling took several minutes to revive him, but within minutes of recovering McClean was writhing on the ground having been bundled down by Chester's Colin Woodthorpe who was fortunate not to be booked. City then pulled their defence together while left-winger Brian Croft, twice a transfer target for Francis, began to spread a little uneasiness in Rovers' back-four with his tricky positive running. In the 33rd minute Croft switched to the other flank to set up Chester's goal from a free-kick lashed in past Brian Parkin from 25 yards by full-back Alan Reeves. Two minutes before half-time McClean should have been credited with a second goal, after Carl Saunders headed on a Twentyman free-kick which brushed Billy Stewart's fingers and rolled towards the line. McClean rushed forward to force the ball in to the goal as Martin Lane lunged despairingly at him. However, the referee penalised McClean who he considered had pushed defenders who were trying to clear.

At 2–1 Chester were still in the game and after surviving early pressure from Rovers at the start of the second half kept their chances very much even. Croft kept burrowing away on his wing but then Gerry Francis pulled off another of his tactical moves, replacing Andy Reece – a player going into suspension – with Devon White to lead the attack with McClean going wide on the right. McClean's third goalbound effort was stopped by his co-striker, when an 82nd-minute shot from the right edge of the box struck Saunders and rebounded to safety.

With Gerry Francis being named as the Third Division's 'Manager of the Month' and a fourth win in eight days Rovers had plenty to celebrate. The sixth successive win by 2–1 was Rovers' eighteenth game without defeat and the unbeaten home run stretched back 28 games to February 1989 eclipsing the run of 27 set up under manager Bert Tann in 1952/53.

## Tuesday 10 April 1990, Leeds Road, Huddersfield

**Huddersfield Town** 1 – Kelly
**Bristol Rovers** 1 – Reece
**Half-time**: 1–1
**Attendance**: 4,359
**Referee**: Neil Midgley (Bolton)
**Huddersfield Town**: Martin, Boothroyd, Hutchings, Kelly, Mitchell, Duggan, O'Regan, May, Byrne, Maskell, Smith. Substitutes: Edwards for Byrne (80 mins), Withe (not used).
**Bristol Rovers**: Parkin, Alexander, Twentyman, Yates, Mehew, Jones, Holloway, Reece, McClean, Saunders, Purnell. Substitutes: White for Purnell (80 mins), Willmott (not used).

Carl Saunders was aiming to end his goal drought at Huddersfield, as the £70,000 signing from Stoke City, who had made a dramatic impression when he arrived at Rovers, scoring 6 goals in his first 5 games, had since failed to hit the net in 9 appearances. However it had not affected Rovers' form as they extended their unbeaten run to 18 games. Manager Francis named the same team which beat Chester, with Andy Reece making his last appearance before the start of a 3-match suspension. Huddersfield, third in the table in February, were now unlikely to even make the Play-offs with five successive home defeats behind them. The Terriers included a young Adrian Boothroyd, a future Rovers signing, in his debut season at full-back and the former Nottingham Forest and Aston Villa European Cup winner Peter Withe as a substitute.

Rovers' defence was jittery from the outset, the normally dependable Geoff Twentyman and Steve Yates indecisive and Ian Alexander mesmerised every time skilful left-winger Mark Smith was in possession. Midfielder John Kelly, on loan from Walsall, had an embarrassingly long time to control Craig Maskell's right-wing cross before prodding a 16th-minute goal over the advancing Brian Parkin. But the home side were unable to punish further errors and Rovers could have been ahead by the break. Carl Saunders was clearly tripped by Graham Mitchell as he turned for goal, but appeals for a penalty were turned down by the referee, and Ian Holloway then saw his left-foot volley well saved by Martin. Then in the final minute of the half, Alexander played a short ball to the by-line to Saunders, who turned it back for Andy Reece to chip the ball astutely past 'keeper Lee Martin into the top corner of the goal from 15 yards.

Carl Saunders should have scored almost from the restart with a left-foot shot from 10 yards with only Martin to beat after Christian McClean had outjumped Andy Duggan to provide the chance, but the striker, who had not scored for five weeks, hit the ball wide of the goalkeeper but against his leg. Rovers' second-half approach was much more positive and they began to dominate the second period. Martin was forced to plunge to his right to keep out Geoff Twentyman's goalbound header from Andy Reece's corner and then Reece himself struck a fierce shot just wide of the post. In the 69th minute McClean jumped well to head Holloway's corner towards goal but it was headed off the line by Town's Kieran O'Regan. And 3 minutes later Rovers came even closer to scoring. Ian Alexander crossed first-time from the right and David Mehew escaped his marker only to see his diving header thump against the outside of a post and rebound to safety.

Despite the preservation of their unbeaten run and remaining handily placed in the second promotion place, with the best defensive record in the country, an angry Gerry Francis pilloried his players for their poor first-half form at Leeds Road. He stormed, 'We have performed magnificently for 37 games this season, but if we play many more like we did in the first 45 minutes, it will all be wasted. This wasn't the Bristol Rovers I know that has reached Wembley and is so high up the league', believing complacency to be a contributing factor, 'But after my half-time chat, we were a different team!'

The Huddersfield Town and Rovers team sheets that were handed to the match referee Neil Midgley.

## Saturday 14 April 1990, Twerton Park

**Bristol Rovers** 2 – Mehew, Jones
**Rotherham United** 0
**Half-time**: 0–0
**Attendance**: 6,794
**Referee**: Michael Pierce (Drayton)
**Bristol Rovers**: Parkin, Alexander, Twentyman, Yates, Mehew, Jones, Holloway, McClean, White, Saunders, Nixon. Substitutes: ) Purnell for Nixon (76 mins), Willmott (not used).
**Rotherham United**: Ford, Pickering, Barnsley, Goodwin, Johnson, Robinson, Buckley, Dempsey, Goater, Mendonca, Pepper. Substitutes: Evans for Dempsey (55 mins), Heard (not used).

The start of the busy Easter period of matches found Rovers out to avenge the New Year's Day 3–2 defeat by Rotherham. Since then, Rovers had only lost once – two weeks later against Brentford – and were looking to stretch their unbeaten run to 20 games against one of only four sides to have claimed 3 points against Rovers all season. The Millers had provided the opponents for Gerry Francis' first game in charge of Rovers on the opening day of the 1987/88 season. But Rovers would have to do it without Andy Reece, who started a three-match suspension, bringing about a recall for Devon White up front with Christian McClean dropping into midfield. Rovers' manager had experimented with this format in the last few games, with McClean playing a wide role and Mehew moving into the centre. Bob Bloomer, who had yet to make his first team debut, was included in the squad.

Full-back Ian Alexander, a former Millers player, had the first scoring opportunity for Rovers when after 14 minutes he latched on to a pass from Mehew and unleashed a right-foot shot from 20 yards which drifted just wide of Ford's right-hand post. Roughed up early on by Rotherham back-four man Ronnie Robinson, Carl Saunders got away from his marker with

Leading goalscorer David Mehew cheers up the Twerton Park faithful with his 19th goal of the season against Rotherham.

Vaughan Jones hits a 25-yard shot to score Rovers' second goal against Rotherham to seal a fine 2–0 victory.

a speedy body swerve to fire a shot that was touched away behind the goal line by debutant goalkeeper Stewart Ford, but the referee awarded a goal-kick. Saunders then went close to sneaking a goal with a suspiciously mishit shot that the agile young 'keeper prised out of the air. In the 26th minute Vaughan Jones lobbed a long ball forward which Saunders pushed past Pickering, but shot wide of Ford and the goal. The former Stoke City striker was then denied a further goalscoring opportunity when he knocked the ball past the Rotherham goalkeeper on the edge of the penalty area only to be floored by Ford when he tried to follow the ball through. The referee decided to play the advantage rule much to the Rovers players' amazement. Gerry Francis was astonished by that and then angered, shortly before half-time, by another decision by first-year referee Mike Pierce who booked Ian Alexander for flooring John Buckley as he started a run 15 yards or so inside his own half.

Francis' half-time briefing included an instruction to Ian Holloway to increase the length of his corner kicks and 4 minutes into the second half he had the chance to do just that. Geoff Twentyman rose to Holloway's corner and directed his header downwards to David Mehew who thrust out his left foot and turned the ball into the net past a number of defenders for his nineteenth goal of the season.

The visitors, having got the better of Rovers earlier in the season, had done their homework and denied Rovers midfield space and shut down on corners, free-kicks and throw-ins – all key areas of Rovers' game. But then Rotherham had to open up their play on falling behind and 5 minutes later Rovers took advantage of the extra space when Mehew's sideways pass in to the path of Vaughan Jones brought a rather special angled 25-yard goal from the full-back. Rovers' captain collected the ball on the edge of the penalty area, sidestepped his marker and struck a shot into the top corner of the goal that gave the goalkeeper no chance.

On the hour the visitors had a chance to get back into the game but a Goater pass threaded through to Mendonca elicited a quick reaction from Brian Parkin to smother the ball at the striker's feet. Saunders then had two chances to score, the first saved by Ford and when the rebound came back to him he fired into the side netting.

Gerry Francis' half-time briefing showed how matches could be won off the field with his instruction to Ian Holloway that broke the deadlock against a side that the Rovers' boss accused of 'wasting as much time as they could'. Carl Saunders' explosive start to his Rovers career – 5 goals in 6 matches – now seemed a long way back as the striker failed to score as Rovers made it 20 league games without being beaten.

## Monday 16 April 1990, St Andrews, Birmingham

**Birmingham City** 2 – Hopkins, Matthewson
**Bristol Rovers** 2 – White, Saunders
**Half-time**: 2–0
**Attendance**: 12,438
**Referee**: Philip Wright (Northwich)
**Birmingham City**: Thomas, Ashley, Overson, Atkins, Matthewson, Frain, Langley, Gleghorn, Bailey, Hopkins, Sturridge. Substitutes: Gordon (not used), Clarkson (not used).
**Bristol Rovers**: Parkin, Jones, Twentyman, Yates, Mehew, Willmott, Holloway, McClean, White, Saunders, Nixon. Substitutes: Purnell for Nixon (67 mins), Hazel for Willmott (87 mins).

Rovers were looking to extend their unbeaten run to 21 games in their Easter Monday clash with Birmingham City, who were still clinging to a faint hope of an end of season play-off place. In addition to missing Andy Reece, midway through a 3-match suspension, defender Ian Alexander was also unavailable serving a 1-match ban. This gave Ian Willmott the chance to come in at left-back with captain Vaughan Jones moving across to the right.

Birmingham played with a swirling, gusting wind behind them and took full advantage of the conditions, whilst Rovers were finding it difficult to cope with the tricky wind as much as Birmingham's play and when the ball deviated wickedly Hopkins darted behind Geoff Twentyman in the 16th minute to head a perfect right-wing cross from Kevin Ashley past Brian Parkin. Four minutes later Nigel Gleghorn's corner was also affected by the blustery

Devon White heads Rovers' first goal after 58 minutes past Birmingham goalkeeper Martin Thomas, a former Rovers custodian.

weather to such an extent that Parkin missed the ball and Trevor Matthewson headed firmly into the net. Rovers' defence – the meanest in the Football League – was in a shambles. Robert Hopkins was denied a penalty in the 29th minute after full-back Ian Willmott brought him down in the penalty area, but the referee ignored one of the most blatant of trips seen during the season and waved play on. Simon Sturridge then missed two easy chances, Brian Parkin finger-tipped another Hopkins shot over the bar and an Ian Atkins header thudded off the crossbar to safety in the final minutes of the half. Christian McClean's header from a Holloway corner which struck goalkeeper Martin Thomas' leg on the goal line and a Paul Nixon header from another Holloway corner that hit a post were all Rovers had to show during a lethargic first half.

The transformation in Rovers in the second half resulted from a combination of the elements and the manager's persuasive powers, encouraging his team to put the ball in the box as often as possible. With a strong wind at their backs, Rovers began the second half in a far more confident mood, and within 12 minutes of the restart Devon White had reduced the arrears. Rovers' rediscovered attacking prowess paid dividends when at full speed he ducked to head in a measured Vaughan Jones cross past goalkeeper Thomas.

Holloway and Mehew both wasted good efforts while at the other end livewire Hopkins was a constant menace to the Rovers back line. With 7 minutes remaining Thomas unwittingly gave his former teammates a hand when he failed to gather a teasing Holloway wind-assisted cross from the right. Springing to his right he misjudged the flight of the ball and dropped it almost on the goal line for Carl Saunders to tap in his first goal for six weeks. Once again Rovers had left it until the last few minutes before they could celebrate another amazing comeback with their many noisy travelling supporters.

Assistant manager Kenny Hibbitt confided to the press after the match that manager Gerry Francis, once again angry with his team's poor first 45 minutes, had given his side the biggest roasting of the season at half-time. 'You couldn't recognise us as a team that has the best defensive record in the country and lost only 4 games', commented Francis who was nonetheless full of praise for yet another second half comeback. Birmingham boss, Dave Mackay, considered the game great entertainment, but 'the game should have been over by half-time,' a view no doubt shared by Gerry Francis. However, Martin Thomas, the former Welsh international who left Rovers for Newcastle United, believed that his old club would win automatic promotion, 'They have proved themselves such a consistent side that I can't see them failing now.'

## Saturday 21 April 1990, Twerton Park

**Bristol Rovers** 1 – White
**Crewe Alexandra** 1 – Cutler
**Half-time**: 0–0
**Attendance**: 7,250
**Referee**: Ffrangcon Roberts (Prestatyn)
**Bristol Rovers**: Parkin, Alexander, Twentyman, Yates, Mehew, Jones, Holloway, McClean, White, Saunders, Nixon. Substitutes: Hazel for McClean (60 mins), Purnell for Nixon (60 mins).
**Crewe Alexandra**: Greygoose, Swain, McKearney, Smart, Jasper, Hignett, Jones, Murphy, Foreman, Sussex, Callaghan. Substitutes: Cutler for Jones (68 mins), Gardiner for Sussex (68 mins).

With 6 league matches remaining Rovers were hoping to extend their unbeaten run to 30 games, but Crewe were unlikely to be impressed by that record. Just before Christmas they ended Rovers' unbeaten run of 14 games with a 1–0 win at Gresty Road. Ian Alexander returned at right-back for Rovers and Crewe included goalkeeper Dean Greygoose who, after a spell with Crystal Palace displacing Brian Parkin, joined them in August 1987.

Geoff Twentyman had an important pre-match message for the Rovers fans flooding to see the Railwaymen's first ever visit to Twerton Park and only the 6th league meeting between the clubs, 'You can play a crucial role in our final home games and we need your support. Our fans are a very important part of the atmosphere at Twerton Park and we need you to get behind us', said the defender, who was passed fit the day before the game following a niggling groin injury.

Crewe, an even more regimented side than Rovers thanks to manager Dario Gradi's revolutionary 4-5-1 formation, spent much of the game camped in their own half with Darren Foreman as a lone striker. And as Rovers kept three defenders back, Crewe had the advantage in midfield and on the fringe of their own penalty area where most of the action took place. Ian Alexander, who popped up all over the field, twice produced crosses which set up good chances for his forwards that they were unable to convert into goals. Carl Saunders was let through by Callaghan, but a hasty shot went straight at goalkeeper Greygoose, and when Paul Nixon headed the ball back into the middle, Devon White side-footed over from 8 yards.

The arrival of Ian Hazel and Phil Purnell in a double substitution on the hour brought fresh hope and enthusiasm and Rovers' goal came after 70 minutes when Crewe were caught out by Ian Holloway's pass to Devon White. The big striker cut in from the left to score his eleventh goal of the season with an angled low cross-shot into the far corner from 12 yards. Crewe, who had also brought on both substitutes, counter-attacked but Brian Parkin only had one difficult save to make diving at Craig Hignett's feet. The visitors' equaliser in the 79th minute followed a dash upfield by Alexander and a centre into the opposition goalkeeper's hands. With Alexander out of position Rovers' defensive discipline was in question as Hignett sped down the left, and White, temporarily filling in as right-back, missed a high bounce and sold himself in a despairing tackle. The ball was switched inside for Chris Cutler to score in the corner past the advancing Parkin. Three minutes from time Carl Saunders worked his way into the penalty area and appeared to be grabbed by Aaron Callaghan, when the Crewe captain ran in front of Rovers' striker and pushed him. Referee 'Frank' Roberts, however, awarded an indirect free-kick for obstruction 15 yards from the goal line which Vaughan Jones blasted at one of the eleven Crewe men stationed behind the ball. White was then penalised for pushing as he headed in a Holloway corner and a Jones free-kick from 20 yards was magnificently touched aside by Greygoose. Even then the visitors might have snatched a winner, but Mark Gardiner's far-post header flashed over the crossbar by inches.

A lack of concentration in defence, leaving only three at the back which cost a goal, combined with poor finishing were instrumental in the loss of 2 precious points in Rovers' promotion quest. Disappointed Rovers manager Gerry Francis lamented, 'We missed a great chance to put pressure on the three other teams at the top,' but his side still stood in 2nd place with a game in hand on their arch-rivals and had extended their unbeaten run to 22 games.

## 21 APRIL 1990

|                    | P  | W  | D  | L  | F  | A  | Pts |
|--------------------|----|----|----|----|----|----|-----|
| Bristol City       | 42 | 26 | 9  | 7  | 71 | 35 | 87  |
| BRISTOL ROVERS     | 41 | 22 | 15 | 4  | 61 | 31 | 81  |
| Tranmere Rovers    | 42 | 23 | 9  | 10 | 82 | 43 | 78  |
| Notts County       | 41 | 22 | 10 | 9  | 62 | 47 | 76  |
| Bury               | 43 | 19 | 11 | 13 | 66 | 48 | 68  |
| Bolton Wanderers   | 42 | 17 | 13 | 12 | 56 | 44 | 64  |
| Birmingham City    | 43 | 17 | 12 | 14 | 57 | 55 | 63  |

## Monday 23 April 1990, Prenton Park, Birkenhead

**Tranmere Rovers** 1 – Muir
**Bristol Rovers** 2 – Twentyman, Holloway (penalty)
**Half-time**: 1– 0
**Attendance**: 12,723
**Referee**: David Allison (Lancaster)
**Tranmere Rovers**: Nixon, Vickers, Hughes, Higgins, Thomas, Harvey, McNab, Malkin, Mungall, Muir, Steel. Substitutes: Fairclough for Hughes (73 mins), Bishop for Harvey (80 mins).
**Bristol Rovers**: Parkin, Alexander, Twentyman, Yates, Mehew, Jones, Holloway, Reece, White, Saunders, Nixon. Substitutes: McClean for Nixon (61 mins), Hazel for Saunders (89 mins).

Rovers began the final push for Division Two with a trip to Birkenhead against one of their main promotion rivals, 3rd-placed Tranmere Rovers, followed a week after by a tough visit to Notts County and a penultimate fixture against the league leaders – Bristol City. Rival promotion managers, John King and Neil Warnock, interviewed in the *Bristol Evening Post* warned that Tranmere and County were ready to spoil the Bristol double promotion dream. Leaders Bristol City needed 6 points to clinch promotion, and Warnock felt that 'Bristol City will walk it. I think they've been the best all season,' although Tranmere's boss, King, did not accept that the Robins were running away with it – and neither did Gerry Francis.

Rovers were soon behind in the vital promotion clash, almost inevitably trailing to a goal that should have been prevented, when a moment of madness by Brian Parkin led to Tranmere's 11th-minute opener. He charged outside the penalty area to try and head clear a long through ball that had bypassed the Rovers defence. In the tangle, the ball fell for Chris Malkin, but his right-footed shot from just inside the box was expertly blocked on the six-yard line by Steve Yates. Unluckily for Rovers, the ball fell to Tranmere's top scorer Ian Muir whose finish past Alexander's desperate lunge was perfect. Rovers almost levelled within 4 minutes when a Vaughan Jones free-kick was turned against a post by goalkeeper Eric Nixon, who somehow managed to recover to make an instinctive save when David Mehew met the rebound.

The equaliser came in the 63rd minute after Christian McClean, who had replaced Paul Nixon 2 minutes earlier, and Devon White rose to meet a Vaughan Jones free-kick taken from deep inside Rovers' half of the field. As Mehew and Saunders challenged for the loose ball it broke to the left and Geoff Twentyman's left-foot shot from 20 yards took a deflection over Eric Nixon as it bobbled into the far corner of the goal. Tranmere, sensing that their chance of an automatic promotion spot was receding, launched a late rally. Skipper Jimmy Harvey blasted a shot over the crossbar. Parkin then saved well from Ian Muir and when Steve Vickers centred across the goal area Steel had a close-range shot deflected away. Although Tranmere looked dangerous in counter-attacks, Twentyman and Yates were usually in control. Rovers always looked comfortable and confident of getting a draw and content to extend an unbeaten record to 23 games, until the 86th minute. Vaughan Jones' throw-in from the left touch-line was allowed to run on by Carl Saunders and as he advanced on goal was tripped on the edge of the penalty area by Dave Higgins and sent tumbling by Steve Mungall as he fell inside the box. Referee David Allison ruled that the initial tackle had taken place in the box and pointed to the penalty spot. The moment demanded a cool, calculating approach as Pirates fans cheered and Tranmere followers booed. More disconcerting was the delay while Saunders received treatment and Tony Thomas was booked for protesting. Ian Holloway, nursing an injured right knee, stroked the penalty decisively to Eric Nixon's left, as the goalkeeper dived to his right, for his sixth league goal of the season. His goal meant a record-equalling tenth away win for the second successive season.

Rovers played with panache and composure with the immaculate Vaughan Jones, energetic Ian Alexander and the ceaseless midfield endeavours of Ian Holloway and Andy Reece which kept Tranmere back-pedalling. Devon White probably won 90 per cent of balls in the air, while the speed and guile of Saunders was a persistent threat to the home defence. Rovers' fans sang 'Goodnight Irene' with all the gusto of the clubs' halcyon days at Eastville as Tranmere's dejected followers filed silently into the Merseyside night. The West Country contingent was in no doubt that promotion was now a formality after a magnificent display of skill, commitment and determination at Prenton Park, and manager Gerry Francis emerged later to applaud the fans for their loyal support.

## Thursday 26 April 1990, Meadow Lane, Nottingham

**Notts County** 3 – Johnson 2 (1 penalty), Turner
**Bristol Rovers** 1 – Mehew
**Half-time**: 1–0
**Attendance**: 10,142
**Referee**: Vic Callow (Shirley)
**Notts County**: Cherry, Palmer, Platnauer, Short, Yates, Robinson, Thomas, Turner, Bartlett, Lund, Johnson. Substitutes: Norton (not used), Stant (not used).
**Bristol Rovers**: Parkin, Alexander, Twentyman, Yates, Mehew, Jones, Holloway, Reece, White, Saunders, McClean. Substitutes: Nixon for Reece (56 mins), Hazel (not used).

Rovers stuck to the regular morning routine in preparation for the latest instalment of the promotion showdown, which meant a good hour's running around for Gerry Francis' squad before departing for Nottingham. Quite apart from the physical benefits, there was also a hint of superstition about sticking to a successful formula. The Pirates had gone 23 matches unbeaten in their march towards a promotion and Leyland Daf Cup double and were in 2nd place with 84 points, with County third and 79 points – both had played 42 games. The Magpies, boosted by their biggest league crowd of the season, had not only promotion in their sights, but were seeking revenge for Rovers' Leyland Daf Cup victory earlier in the month.

Rovers made the early running and won a pair of corners, but both were hit too high for target-man Devon White. County's Tommy Johnson put in Bartlett and central defender Steve Yates slipped to allow Lund a clear strike at goal, but his first-time shot just went wide. It was Gary Lund again who forced Brian Parkin to concede a corner when he tried an acrobatic scissors kick which was tipped wide. Both Thomas and Robinson came close as Notts forced three corners within 2 minutes and it seemed just a matter of time before they opened the scoring. The goal duly came in the 15th minute. County's skipper Phil Turner put Johnson through on the left, the youngster held up play and passed inside to Thomas on the edge of the area, who slotted a first-time ball through to his captain to fire into the roof of the net with his left foot from an acute angle. County were looking to full-backs Charlie Palmer and Nicky Platnauer to move forward, while the less subtle visitors were content with a string of high, hopeful balls which were causing Yates and Short little trouble. And when Carl Saunders was about to latch onto a through ball, the rangy stride of Dean Yates enabled him to chase back with a vital sliding tackle. Rovers enjoyed possession, but failed to make the most of their openings and their best first-half chances came from a long-range Alexander strike which went for a corner off a defender plus a 44th-minute shot from Devon White which was deflected away at the near-post.

Gerry Francis' men were out a good 2 minutes before the restart, but it was County who made the better start to the second half. Lund shot wide after doing well to make space and Johnson might have done better when a Thomas ball put him through. There was an even better chance for the forward when Steve Cherry's goal kick bounced over the Rovers' defence, but it fell on his weaker right foot and although he lobbed Parkin the shot had little power and Steve Yates was able to clear off the line. Paul Nixon came on for midfielder Ian Holloway and was immediately in the thick of things, hitting a 10-yard shot which was pushed away for a corner. Johnson moved onto the County right flank, and latched onto an accurate ball from Lund to cross to Bartlett who had found space, but he shot straight at the 'keeper.

It was a disappointing effort but Bartlett made amends after 66 minutes with an unselfish bit of play to set up Johnson's first goal. He ran onto a miskicked clearance from Twentyman and avoided Vaughan Jones' desperate tackle before drawing the 'keeper and passing to Johnson, who merely tapped into the empty net. Rovers were short of inspiration and Christian McClean was booked when he began arguing with the referee who had given a free-kick for a foul on Nicky Platnauer. A long ball in from Alexander appeared to catch Cherry unawares, and as the former Derby 'keeper back-pedalled he was relieved to see the ball go over. But with 10 minutes remaining Rovers pulled a goal back. Devon White won the ball from Short and when his through-ball found Mehew free on the left of the box, the midfielder looked up before hitting an inch-perfect chip over Cherry, to send the large visiting support wild. That seemed to stimulate Rovers and County had Platnauer to thank for clearing a McClean shot off the line after a goal-mouth melee. It was a worrying time for County supporters and they breathed a collective sigh of relief when Johnson made the game safe with a penalty 5 minutes from time. The tricky Bartlett was pulled down by a combination of Yates and Holloway and Johnson side-footed the penalty inches beyond Parkin's right hand.

Jubilant Magpies manager Neil Warnock praised his team after a fighting display which kept them in the hunt for automatic promotion from Division Three, having witnessed his side's second vital win in forty-eight hours. County's 3–1 defeat of Rovers at Meadow Lane took them within 2 points of the Pirates who remained in 2nd place, with both sides having 3 games left. Rovers' boss Gerry Francis on seeing his side's 23-match unbeaten run ended in such convincing fashion commented:

> Notts deserved to win and I was disappointed with the all-round performance of my players. This was not a different Notts side from the one we beat in the Leyland Daf; they just wanted it more on the night. The defeat hasn't lost us promotion or won Notts promotion. If we win all our remaining games we're up and it's as simple as that.

## Saturday 28 April 1990, Twerton Park

**Bristol Rovers** 1 – Holloway (penalty)
**Shrewsbury Town** 0
Half-time: 1–0
Attendance: 7,903
Referee: Peter Tyldesley (Stockport)
**Bristol Rovers**: Parkin, Alexander, Twentyman, Yates, Mehew, Jones, Holloway, Reece, White, Saunders, Purnell. Substitutes: McClean for White (80 mins), Nixon for Purnell (80 mins).
**Shrewsbury Town**: Perks, Worsley, Moyes, Blake, Gorman, Brown, Kelly, Wimbleton, Naughton, Spink, Melrose. Substitutes: Weir for Naughton (69 mins), Parrish for Wimbleton (80 mins).

After the disappointing end to Rovers' twenty-three match unbeaten run on Thursday night, the home game with Shrewsbury took on even greater significance in what could prove to be the Twerton Park side's greatest test of character. Playing their fourth game in eight days, Rovers needed to display the strength and character to sustain a Second Division challenge, but as Gerry Francis emphatically reassured, 'We haven't lost 2 consecutive games for two seasons and don't intend starting now.' After missing the vital clashes with Tranmere and Notts County through injury Phil Purnell returned to the Rovers side. Shrewsbury included future Bristol City defender and Everton manager David Moyes, and Paul Wimbleton, who had already made 2 appearances against Rovers at Ashton Gate when with City.

Phil Purnell might have signalled his return with an early goal after 6 minutes when he picked the ball up on the left from a defensive clearance, cut inside two defenders on a run which took him into the penalty area and fired in a fierce cross-shot from the edge of the eighteen-yard box. But Perks in the Shrewsbury goal dived full length to his left to tip the

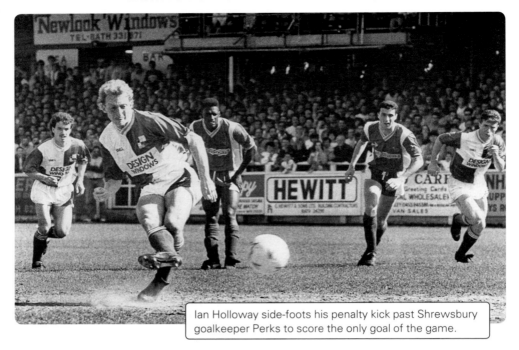

Ian Holloway side-foots his penalty kick past Shrewsbury goalkeeper Perks to score the only goal of the game.

ball round the post for a corner. Rovers continued to press and in the 21st-minute Holloway fired a long-range shot straight at Perks, which the goalkeeper collected comfortably, before David Mehew was a whisker away from opening the scoring. Ian Alexander, just inside his own half, had spotted space behind the Shrewsbury defence and launched the ball forward. Both Mehew and Devon White outstripped the Shrews defenders, but it was Mehew who reached the ball to cleverly lob it over the advancing goalkeeper from the edge of the box. Mark Blake, running back, just managed to hook the goal-bound shot off the goal line. In the 33rd minute Alexander, on another of his forward runs down the right, pushed the ball wide to Holloway who did well to keep the ball in play. His right-footed cross into the penalty area found Carl Saunders who stumbled and fell as Graeme Worsley attempted to challenge. The referee instantly awarded a penalty despite the protestations of the Shrewsbury defender who claimed Rovers' striker had tripped over his own heel. Holloway stepped up to side-foot the spot-kick to the goalkeeper's left as Perks moved the other way, for his 7th league goal of the season. Purnell had a good opportunity to double Rovers' lead in the 37th minute when the Shrewsbury goalkeeper, under pressure from Mehew, could only punch the ball clear to the winger, who mishit his shot wide of the goal with Perks still off his line.

In the second half Shrewsbury continued their boring offside trap, and showed few imaginative ideas, with Brian Parkin not having to save one shot behind a defence that was seldom under pressure. Devon White, so effectively shadowed by David Moyes, was slow reacting to one shooting chance, and Mehew had a volley turned aside by Perks near the end. In the 84th minute Saunders set up Paul Nixon on the left and when the substitute cut inside his shot from just outside the penalty area was fumbled by Perks and turned around the post for a corner.

Rovers appeared tired and jaded in their fourth game in eight days, following the acute disappointment of losing at Notts County, but they were soon buoyed by the news of Bristol City's 1–0 defeat at Bolton and Notts County's 1–1 draw at Wigan. The several hundred fans who invaded the Twerton Park pitch after the victory were in no doubt that Rovers were going up, but the cheers and calls for the players and Gerry Francis to join the celebrations were premature, as 2 more points were still required to ensure promotion, and there was the small matter of a Bristol derby on Wednesday night.

## 28 APRIL 1990

|  | P | W | D | L | F | A | Pts |
|---|---|---|---|---|---|---|---|
| Bristol City | 44 | 26 | 10 | 8 | 72 | 37 | 88 |
| BRISTOL ROVERS | 44 | 24 | 15 | 5 | 65 | 35 | 87 |
| Notts County | 44 | 24 | 11 | 9 | 68 | 50 | 83 |
| Tranmere Rovers | 44 | 23 | 9 | 12 | 84 | 47 | 78 |
| Bury | 45 | 20 | 11 | 14 | 68 | 49 | 71 |
| Bolton Wanderers | 44 | 18 | 13 | 13 | 57 | 46 | 67 |
| Birmingham City | 45 | 18 | 12 | 15 | 60 | 58 | 66 |

## Wednesday 2 May 1990, Twerton Park

Bristol Rovers 3 – White 2, Holloway (penalty)
Bristol City 0
Half-time: 1–0
Attendance: 9,813
Referee: Lawrence Dilkes (Mossley)
Bristol Rovers: Parkin, Alexander, Twentyman, Yates, Mehew, Jones, Holloway, Reece, White, Saunders, Purnell. Substitutes: McClean (not used), Nixon (not used).
Bristol City: Sinclair, Llewellyn, Humphries, Newman, Bailey, Shelton, Gavin, Rennie, Morgan, Turner, Smith. Substitutes: Honor for Bailey (62 mins), Ferguson for Turner (75 mins).

The rearranged derby match had originally been set for 3 February, when City had four straight wins behind them while Rovers had two draws and two defeats in their previous 4 league matches. Rovers were now in a far better vein of form than their neighbours, with just one defeat in their last

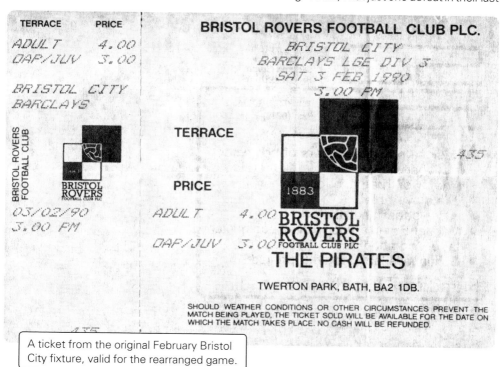

A ticket from the original February Bristol City fixture, valid for the rearranged game.

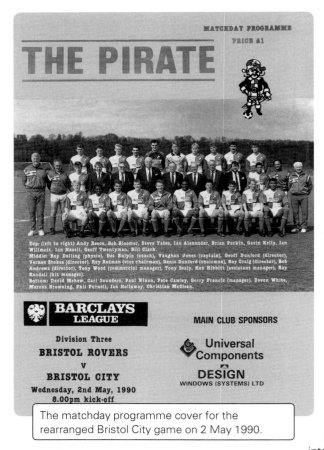

MATCHDAY PROGRAMME
PRICE £1

THE PIRATE

Top: (left to right) Andy Reece, Bob Bloomer, Steve Yates, Ian Alexander, Brian Parkin, Gavin Kelly, Ian Willmott, Ian Hazell, Geoff Twentyman, Bill Clark.
Middle: Roy Dolling (physio), Des Bulpin (coach), Vaughan Jones (captain), Geoff Dunford (director), Vernon Stokes (director), Roy Redman (vice chairman), Denis Dunford (chairman), Roy Craig (director), Bob Andrews (director), Tony Wood (commercial manager), Tony Sealy, Ken Hibbitt (assistant manager), Ray Kendall (kit manager).
Bottom: David Mehew, Carl Saunders, Paul Nixon, Pete Cawley, Gerry Francis (manager), Devon White, Marcus Browning, Phil Purnell, Ian Holloway, Christian McClean.

**BARCLAYS LEAGUE**

Division Three
**BRISTOL ROVERS**
v
**BRISTOL CITY**
Wednesday, 2nd May, 1990
8.00pm kick-off

MAIN CLUB SPONSORS

**Universal Components**

**DESIGN**
WINDOWS (SYSTEMS) LTD

The matchday programme cover for the rearranged Bristol City game on 2 May 1990.

20 league games. In contrast, City had spluttered of late, with two draws and a defeat in their last 3 matches.

However, there was more at stake that just 3 points, and local status and pride in what *Western Daily Press* reporter David Foot described as, 'probably the most crucial soccer match ever between the two Bristol clubs'. City would clinch the Third Division title if they won, but would still be sure of promotion with 1 point. Rovers needed 3 points to ensure promotion, but if Notts County failed to take maximum points at Reading on Thursday night both Bristol clubs would be sure of going up.

Gerry Francis gave his players a rigorous training session on the Tuesday but allowed them the morning off on the day of the match. He believed that his team's ability to handle pressure would help them overcome City in the promotion battle. It was the first time Rovers had gone into a game with the chance to clinch promotion with a win, whereas, 'City had had that for 2 games and didn't appear to have enjoyed it,' commented the Rovers boss. City's Bob Taylor was ruled out of the derby game with a hamstring injury which had flared up in the 1–0 defeat at Bolton, with ex-Rover Robbie Turner returning to the attack for his first game since the end of March.

On the evening of 2 May a record Twerton Park crowd of 9,813 was packed into the tiny home that Rovers shared with Bath City in the match that was the defining moment of the 1989/90 season. Rovers kicked off playing towards the massed ranks of City fans at the Bristol End, but Mark Gavin had the first chance of the night after 3 minutes, when Robbie Turner flicked on a John Bailey free-kick and the winger found space on the right edge of the box only to fire across goal and wide. In the 16th minute Rovers carved out a chance with Andy Reece starting and finishing the move. Devon White laid Holloway's pass off to the busy midfielder but he shot wide from close range. The advantage went to Rovers just past the midway point of the first half when Devon White opened the scoring. Carl Saunders hit a long cross-field ball to an unmarked David Mehew, who had made good ground down the right flank, and Rovers' leading scorer crossed first-time into the 6-yard box. Cleared by the City defence, but only as far as Mehew, his second cross eluded defender Andy Llewellyn to reach Devon White, who deftly controlled the ball before stabbing it past Ronnie Sinclair into the left corner of the goal.

The goal allowed Rovers to settle and play some thoughtful football, all the more impressive considering promotion was at stake. Rovers created two more chances just after their opener. Reece played a long ball into the area and Phil Purnell met it with a header which went narrowly wide in the 27th minute, and then Saunders held up a Vaughan Jones free-kick and played it back to Holloway steaming in, but the midfielder drove just over. There was a scare in the Rovers goalmouth a minute before the interval, when Ian Alexander's backpass to his 'keeper fell short and Shelton got in a shot, but the Rovers full-back managed to make amends by blocking it and also headed away Turner's follow up.

Gerry Francis' side clearly had their opponents on the back foot at the break, and they piled on the pressure after the restart. In the 49th minute Carl Saunders nodded just wide of Sinclair's goal from an Ian Alexander cross from the right following good work by Mehew. Turner had a chance for City 3 minutes into the second half, when Gavin found him with a deep cross but the striker powered his header across goal and wide. Dave Rennie had a similar chance to get the Robins back in the game in the 51st minute. Dave Smith crossed from the right after dashing on to Gavin's pass, but Brian Parkin read the unmarked Rennie's well directed header to make an acrobatic catch by his left-hand post. Almost immediately Devon White collected the ball after Glenn Humphries' poor control near the left touchline gave the ball away to Rovers' scorer. The ball was knocked into Saunders in the penalty area who took it wide to the left leaving Newman floundering as the defender slipped as he attempted to tackle and Saunders unselfishly laid the ball into the path of the advancing Devon White who coolly side-footed the ball under Bailey's outstretched leg and wide of Sinclair's dive into the far corner of the goal.

In the 58th minute goalkeeper Ronnie Sinclair failed to hold a high cross from Ian Alexander when challenged by David Mehew and the ball eventually ran free to Phil Purnell just inside the box. Purnell's goal-bound shot, with Sinclair still absent from his goal, was handled on the line by Andy Llewellyn and as the ball popped up was headed into the empty goal by David Mehew. However, the referee's whistle had already blown before Mehew had 'scored' and Lawrence Dilkes awarded a penalty-kick. The referee then halted play as police battled to keep City fans in their enclosure, order being finally restored when City manager Joe Jordan stood in a line of police to plead with the minority to behave. Using a megaphone, Jordan eventually calmed the crowd but spent the rest of the match near the corner flag. After a 4-minute delay, whilst City fans were causing a disturbance in the visitors' end, Ian Holloway

From a Carl Saunders' pass, Devon White side-foots Rovers' second goal against the Robins.

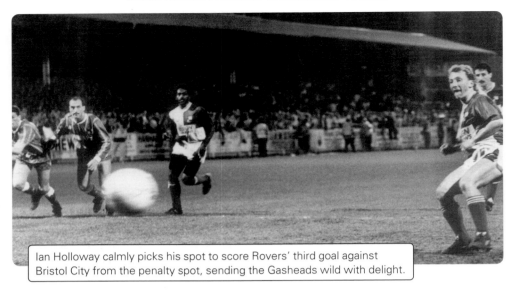

Ian Holloway calmly picks his spot to score Rovers' third goal against Bristol City from the penalty spot, sending the Gasheads wild with delight.

calmly converted the spot-kick, driving the ball to Sinclair's right, the goalkeeper committed himself in the opposite direction, to wild scenes of delight on three sides of Twerton Park.

Rovers had a chance to increase their goal tally after 66 minutes when Phil Purnell crossed from the left for Devon White to direct a header down to Carl Saunders just inside the penalty area. The striker deftly turned past his marker and fired in a shot only for Sinclair to grasp his goalbound effort.

The Bristol Rovers promotion party ended in highly emotional scenes as thousands ran on to the pitch to acclaim their heroes. Jubilant Rovers supporters swarmed from the terraces at the final whistle as the players dashed for the safety of the dressing room. But within 2 minutes the team emerged clutching bottles of champagne to lead their followers in song and joke with the thousands chanting and waving their arms. Despite unrest among the City fans behind the goal that briefly threatened to cause abandonment, Rovers won 3–0 to go top of the Third Division for the first time since Boxing Day and secure Division Two football for the first time since 1980/81. Remarkably the result also meant that Rovers had completed the season without a single home defeat in the league.

Gerry Francis put the incredible achievement into perspective, 'I had 11 free transfers in my 13 for tonight's game and what they have achieved is virtually impossible to put into words. I don't think in this club's history they have achieved anything as good as this,' said the Rovers boss; 'To go through the season with only five defeats is remarkable and only Liverpool can match that and they have played 37 games – this was our 45th.' And both Bristol clubs still had one match to play to decide the championship.

## 3 MAY 1990

|  | P | W | D | L | F | A | Pts |
|---|---|---|---|---|---|---|---|
| BRISTOL ROVERS | 45 | 25 | 15 | 5 | 68 | 35 | 90 |
| Bristol City | 45 | 26 | 10 | 9 | 72 | 40 | 88 |
| Notts County | 45 | 24 | 12 | 9 | 69 | 51 | 84 |
| Tranmere Rovers | 45 | 23 | 10 | 12 | 84 | 47 | 79 |
| Bury | 45 | 20 | 11 | 14 | 68 | 49 | 71 |
| Bolton Wanderers | 45 | 18 | 14 | 13 | 59 | 48 | 68 |
| Birmingham City | 45 | 18 | 12 | 15 | 60 | 58 | 66 |

## Saturday 5 May 1990, Bloomfield Road, Blackpool

Blackpool 0
Bristol Rovers 3 – Mehew, Purnell, Nixon
Half-time: 0–0
Attendance: 7,250
Referee: Robert Nixon (West Kirby)
Blackpool: Wood, Davies, Matthews, Methven, Morgan, Groves, Gouck, Sinclair, Owen, Brook, Eyres. Substitutes: Garner for Groves (62 mins), Bradshaw for Owen (67 mins).
Bristol Rovers: Parkin, Alexander, Twentyman, Yates, Mehew, Jones, Holloway, Reece, White, Saunders, Purnell. Substitutes: Nixon for Purnell (77 mins), McClean (not used).

Rovers' players travelled to Blackpool on Friday staying overnight in one of the seaside resort's hotels, it being the only away fixture of the season which they travelled to a game the day before. Victory at Blackpool would clinch the Division Three Championship, but even if the win was achieved Rovers would have to wait to receive the trophy as the Football League was not keen on presenting it at away matches. Originally it was anticipated that if Rovers won the trophy it would be presented the following Friday at Vaughan Jones' testimonial game against Tottenham, but Spurs were no longer available to play the match.

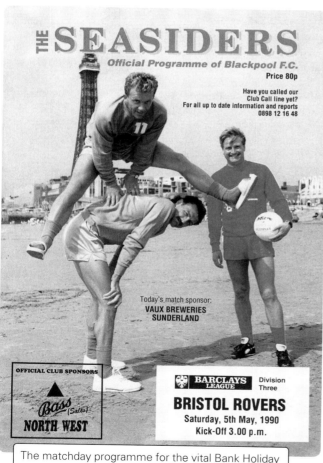

The matchday programme for the vital Bank Holiday clash with Blackpool at Bloomfield Road.

And, of course, Bristol City could still claim the title if they won their remaining fixture and the Pirates were defeated at Bloomfield Road.

Gerry Francis selected the same team and substitutes that had gained the club promotion on the 2 May, while Blackpool's acting manager Tom White, who took over when Jimmy Mullen resigned in April, was without his first choice centre-backs Shaun Elliot and Gary Briggs, both injured. Thousands of Rovers fans made the journey north to take over Bloomfield Road on a hot Bank Holiday weekend to create a carnival atmosphere. The kick-off was delayed for 10 minutes to make sure that every Rovers fan was present in the ground and a deafening crescendo greeted the players' arrival on the pitch while Gerry Francis, his assistant Kenny Hibbitt, physiotherapist Roy Dolling and kit man Ray Kendall smiled and waved.

Blackpool goalkeeper George Wood is beaten by Phil Purnell's shot just before half-time, to put Rovers two goals up.

David Mehew opened the scoring in the 28th minute with his 21st goal of the season after Phil Purnell was fouled just outside the box and Mehew rose to head in Vaughan Jones' free-kick from the left with one of those late runs that he had made so often during the season. Phil Purnell scored a second goal a minute before half-time when Andy Reece carved open the Blackpool defence with a magnificent 50-yard pass and Purnell raced down the left from the halfway line to calmly beat goalkeeper George Wood with a right-foot shot.

The Rovers fans – some with faces painted blue and white, others wearing an assortment of hats and curly wigs – ringed the touchline during the final 5 minutes. The chanting, clapping, cheering fans – packed in the Kop End and along one side – outnumbered home followers by four to one and sang out the obligatory 'Goodnight Irene', a chorus of

Substitute Paul Nixon scores Rovers' third goal against Blackpool, the Pirates' final league goal of their championship season.

Some of the 5,000 supporters who took over Bloomfield Road celebrate the 3–0 victory which gave Rovers the Third Division championship.

'You'll Never Walk Alone', and 'We are the Champions'. This was confirmed when substitute Paul Nixon volleyed a third goal from 20 yards, 2 minutes from time. Following good play down the right by Mehew, Devon White crossed left-footed to the edge of the penalty area where Nixon controlled the ball at the second attempt and struck his right-foot shot past Wood in the Blackpool goal.

Rovers fans poured onto the pitch hugging their heroes, each other and even the Blackpool players, who could only look on bemused. But it was all good natured enjoyment though it took some minutes before the pitch was cleared. Hidden among the crush was manager Gerry Francis, who abandoned the dug-out and was vainly trying to see what was happening on the pitch, as the faithful queued up to shake his hand and pat him on the back. Finally, the

Rovers players celebrate the end of the successful league season in a carnival atmosphere at Blackpool.

referee blew his whistle to signal the end of the match and the start of the real celebrations as the Rovers players sprinted off the pitch pursued by admirers. Club officials confirmed 5,000 fans had made the journey from Bristol and it seemed like every one of them was on the pitch waiting for their heroes.

And the moment they had all been anticipating finally arrived as Francis and the team emerged in the Directors' Box. He joined in the celebrations grabbing a microphone to conduct and lead the singing and chanting from the stand wearing a pirate's hat. And afterwards Francis admitted it was one of the most satisfying days of his football career. In the boardroom, the Blackpool directors opened champagne to toast Rovers' success. They could afford it as visiting fans had given them a £15,000 bonus at the gate.

Blackpool, destined for the Fourth Division, had not spoiled the party as Rovers completed their league programme with a record of only one defeat in the final 28 games and crowned an extraordinary season at Bloomfield Road. The title was theirs and Vaughan Jones became only the second Rovers captain to lift the Division Three championship trophy, emulating Ray Warren in 1953.

## FINAL TABLE

|  | P | W | D | L | F | A | Pts |
|---|---|---|---|---|---|---|---|
| BRISTOL ROVERS | 46 | 26 | 15 | 5 | 71 | 35 | 93 |
| Bristol City | 46 | 27 | 10 | 9 | 76 | 40 | 91 |
| Notts County | 46 | 25 | 12 | 9 | 73 | 53 | 87 |
| Tranmere Rovers | 46 | 23 | 11 | 12 | 86 | 49 | 80 |
| Bury | 46 | 21 | 11 | 14 | 70 | 49 | 74 |
| Bolton Wanderers | 46 | 18 | 15 | 13 | 59 | 48 | 69 |
| Birmingham City | 46 | 18 | 12 | 16 | 60 | 59 | 66 |

## 1989/90 League Appearances
(substitute appearances in brackets)

| Ian Holloway | 46 |
|---|---|
| Vaughan Jones | 46 |
| David Mehew | 46 |
| Geoff Twentyman | 46 |
| Ian Alexander | 43 |
| Andy Reece | 43 |
| Steve Yates | 42 |
| Devon White | 40 (3) |
| Brian Parkin | 30 |
| Paul Nixon | 21 (6) |
| Carl Saunders | 19 (1) |
| Phil Purnell | 17 (5) |
| Nigel Martyn | 16 |
| Ian Willmott | 14 (3) |
| Tony Sealy | 12 (7) |
| Gary Penrice | 12 |
| Christian McClean | 10 (5) |
| Ian Hazel | 2 (6) |
| Peter Cawley | 1 (2) |
| David Byrne | 0 (2) |
| Marcus Browning | 0 (1) |

## League Goalscorers

| David Mehew | 18 |
|---|---|
| Devon White | 12 |
| Ian Holloway | 8 |
| Carl Saunders | 6 |
| Paul Nixon | 5 |
| Christian McClean | 4 |
| Gary Penrice | 3 |
| Tony Sealy | 3 |
| Geoff Twentyman | 3 |
| Vaughan Jones | 2 |
| Phil Purnell | 2 |
| Andy Reece | 2 |
| Ian Alexander | 1 |
| Own goal (Quow) | 1 |
| Own goal (Vickers) | 1 |

## Substitutions:

| Player | Named as sub. | Apps as sub. | Replacing |
|---|---|---|---|
| Peter Cawley | 24 | 2 | (Alexander, Willmott) |
| Ian Willmott | 18 | 3 | (Alexander, Holloway, Purnell) |
| Tony Sealy | 13 | 7 | (Nixon twice , Saunders twice , Mehew, Penrice, Reece) |
| Christian McClean | 11 | 5 | (Hazel twice, Nixon twice, White) |
| Ian Hazel | | 7 | 6 (Nixon twice, Willmott twice, McClean, Saunders) |
| Paul Nixon | 7 | 6 | (Penrice twice, Purnell twice, Reece, Sealy) |
| Phil Purnell | 5 | 5 | (Nixon 4 times, Sealy) |
| Devon White | 3 | 3 | (Reece twice, Purnell) |
| David Byrne | 2 | 2 | (Mehew, Purnell) |
| Marcus Browning | 1 | 1 | (Nixon) |
| Carl Saunders | 1 | 1 | (Nixon) |

## 1989/90 Leyland Daf Appearances and Goals (substitute appearances in brackets)

| Player | Apps | Goals |
|---|---|---|
| Ian Alexander | 8 | |
| Ian Holloway | 8 | 2 |
| Vaughan Jones | 8 | |
| David Mehew | 8 | 2 |
| Andy Reece | 8 | |
| Geoff Twentyman | 8 | |
| Steve Yates | 8 | |
| Brian Parkin | 7 | |
| Phil Purnell | 6 | |
| Devon White | 6 | 2 |
| Carl Saunders | 4 | 1 |
| Paul Nixon | 3 (3) | 1 |
| Tony Sealy | 3 (1) | 1 |
| Christian McClean | 2 (2) | |
| Nigel Martyn | 1 | |
| Marcus Browning | 0 (1) | |
| David Byrne | 0 (1) | |

## Division Three Top Goalscorers 1989/90

| | |
|---|---|
| Bob Taylor (Bristol City) | 27 |
| Dean Holdsworth (Brentford) | 24 |
| Ian Muir (Tranmere Rovers) | 23 |
| John McGinlay (Shrewsbury Town) | 22 |
| Bobby Williamson (Rotherham United) | 19 |
| Dennis Bailey (Birmingham City) | 18 |
| Bobby Barnes (Northampton Town) | 18 |
| Tommy Johnson (Notts County) | 18 |
| **DAVID MEHEW (BRISTOL ROVERS)** | 18 |
| Tony Philliskirk (Bolton Wanderers) | 18 |
| Chris Pike (Cardiff City) | 18 |

Bristol Rovers players, officials and their families begin their open-topped bus tour from Eastville. The previous day they had clinched the Third Division championship at Blackpool. During a stop on the route Ian Holloway, whilst extolling the Rovers' fans support, uttered the immortal words, 'We've had to put up with some crap from all those shitheads.'

Vaughan Jones holds aloft the Barclays Third Division Championship trophy at Twerton Park.

## Sunday 13 May 1990, Twerton Park. Vaughan Jones Testimonial

**Bristol Rovers** 1 – White
**Gerry Francis All-Stars** 2 – Randall, Curle
**Half time**: 0–0
**Attendance**: 4,786
**Referee**: Roger Milford (Bristol)
**Bristol Rovers**: included Parkin, Alexander, Twentyman, Jones, Reece, Holloway, Bloomer, Nixon, White, Saunders, McClean, Purnell.
**Gerry Francis All Stars**: included Gavin Kelly, Gerry Francis, Keith Curle (Wimbledon), Gary Penrice (Watford), Paul Randall (Bath City), Timmy Parkin (Port Vale), Kenny Hibbitt, Tommy Tynan (Plymouth Argyle), Ian Willmott, Marcus Browning, Ian Hazel.

Over 4,700 fans packed Twerton Park for the final time in an outstanding season, the most successful of 63 of them: most points, fewest defeats, unbeaten at home, most away wins, fewest away defeats. The occasion was Vaughan Jones' testimonial match and the presentation at 5.45 p.m. of the Barclays Third Division Championship trophy, 15 minutes before the kick-off. Rovers' top scorer David Mehew was unable to play due to a slight thigh strain, but the Third Division's manager of the season received ecstatic applause when he emerged to lead his team wearing the club's change white and black kit, despite his late arrival as his car broke down on the M4 near Chippenham.

The players were introduced by announcer Keith Valle before embarking on a joyous lap of honour as a final prelude to the game itself. Gerry Francis, subjected to a chorus of 'Gerry, get your hair cut', showed glimpses of the skill that had adorned the First Division and international scene. Assistant manager Kenny Hibbitt captained the All Stars but within 5 minutes was back in the dressing room having two stitches put in an ankle wound, courtesy of 'Mr Testimonial' Vaughan Jones.

The match gave the club's two most recent signings, loan goalkeeper Gavin Kelly from Hull City and £20,000 Bob Bloomer from Chesterfield a chance to meet the supporters. Kelly made impressive saves and looked capable enough to earn a full contract if Rovers decided

Captain Vaughan Jones receives the Barclays Third Division Championship trophy prior to his testimonial game against Gerry Francis' All-Stars XI.

A crowd of 4,786 turned up for the promotion celebrations. From left to right, back row: Gavin Kelly, Marcus Browning, Ian Willmott, Ian Hazel, Paul Nixon, Steve Yates, Devon White, Brian Parkin, David Mehew, Ian Alexander, Ray Kendall, Kenny Hibbitt, Geoff Twentyman. Front row: Bob Bloomer, Christian McClean, Phil Purnell, Ian Holloway, Vaughan Jones, Carl Saunders, Andy Reece.

Some of the Bristol Rovers' promotion squad 1973/74. From left to right, back row: Wayne Jones, Trevor Jacobs, Ray Kendall, Dick Sheppard, Alan Warboys, Stuart Taylor, Jim Eadie, Lindsay Parsons, Harold Jarman (manager), Bobby Brown. Front row: Colin Dobson, Bruce Bannister, Gordon Fearnley, Peter Aitken, Tom Stanton, Frankie Prince, Graham Day.

a second goalkeeper was needed for the following season. Bloomer laid on a goal for Randall after a goalless first half, and Curle swapped passes with Tynan to flick in the second. Although Devon White scored through a crowded goalmouth to reduce the deficit, the blue-and-whites lost for the first time at Twerton Park for almost two years.

Earlier in the year Rovers paraded their Third Division promotion team at Yate Town's Lodge Road ground on Sunday 8 April; not a sudden attack of complacency as the side in question were the 'Boys of 1974' who had last earned Rovers' Second Division status sixteen years previously.

They were reuniting to play the current team in a testimonial match for Vaughan Jones, one of the few links between the teams as he was then an apprentice at Eastville.

Thirty-seven years after topping Division Three (South), Rovers were crowned Third Division champions in 1989/90 with a club record 93 points. It was a momentous achievement for Gerry Francis' 'Ragbag Rovers' at their temporary home outside Bristol. In securing the Third Division championship, Rovers remained unbeaten at home for the only season in the club's history. There were scares, of

Alan Warboys put the 1973/74 promotion side 1–0 up in Vaughan Jones' testimonial match.

course, with Sealy's last-minute equaliser earning a November draw with ten-man Blackpool and Rovers trailing to Cardiff City before 2 injury-time goals earned an unlikely 2–1 victory. Rovers lost just five times in 46 games, a Division Three record, and equalled the club's tally of 26 league victories in 1952/53. Yet, it was achieved the hard way. Rovers, in fact, trailed at half-time in 3 games and only once scored more than 3 goals in a match. The exceptional game was a 6–1 victory over Wigan Athletic in March, where Carl Saunders, a February signing from Stoke City to replace Gary Penrice, scored the first league hat-trick seen at Twerton Park. With Penrice moving to Watford for £500,000, Rovers were further depleted when Nigel Martyn became Britain's first million-pound goalkeeper, his transfer to Crystal Palace smashing Rovers' club record. One body of opinion said that it appeared that the club had relinquished its ambition to obtain Second Division football, while others agreed the 'hard cash' deal ensured the financial viability of the club's directors' dream of securing a new stadium in Bristol in the foreseeable future.

Even the calmest of Rovers supporters was put on the emotional treadmill as the side, with the scent of promotion in its nostrils, recorded six consecutive 2–1 victories in the run-up to Easter. As Bristol City stuttered, the local derby on 2 May assumed gargantuan proportions. It was certainly not a night for the faint-hearted. A glorious two-goal display from Devon White, one in each half, and a late Holloway penalty sealed the promotion push and Rovers were back in Division Two. A night of high drama before a record home crowd for a game at Twerton Park, 9,831, will live long in the memory. Yet, to ensure that Bristol City, also promoted, could not steal the championship away, victory was essential at already-relegated Blackpool in the final game. Over 5,000 Rovers supporters made the trip to Bloomfield Road, where a second successive 3–0 victory saw Rovers secure the championship in a carnival atmosphere. Vaughan Jones was able to lift the trophy at his own testimonial game a week later.

The side which earned this success was largely that which had shown such potential already. Francis stuck with the tried and tested formula, bringing in Ian Willmott, New Zealand international Paul Nixon and Tony Sealy to play sporadic but crucial roles. Sealy scored twice in the win at Shrewsbury Town in November which took Rovers back to the top of the table, while Nixon's 5 goals included the final one as Rovers sealed the championship at Blackpool in May. It was, however, the experienced hands which held the side together. Twentyman, player of the year Holloway, Mehew, and captain Vaughan Jones were all ever-presents, while Alexander, Yates, Reece and White appeared in over 40 league matches each. It was Mehew's pace and fitness that

Obverse of the Barclays League Division Three winners medal presented to David Mehew. It was produced by Vaughtons Ltd of Birmingham; they were first asked in 1911 by the Football League to manufacture its medals and they have been producing them ever since. The company, established in 1819, made the Summer Olympic commemorative medallions for the Games of the IV Olympiad held in London in 1908.

The reverse of the medal inscribed with the season and player's name.

gave Rovers the appearance of playing 4-4-2 and 4-3-3 at the same time and his willingness to get into the penalty area brought him goals throughout the campaign.

A third of the way through the season there was concern about Rovers' disciplinary record, their worst for years. Matters came to a head when Tony Sealy became the fourth player to be sent off in less than six weeks. Whereas manager Francis was prepared to defend the previous three players dismissed he could find no excuses for Sealy's actions. The experienced recent signing became involved in a free-for-all triggered by a clash between his co-striker Devon White and a Huddersfield defender; a visiting centre-back was felled by a punch and Sealy was sent off. The previous Saturday Devon White was dismissed after collecting two bookings at Chester, Steve Yates received a 3-match ban resulting from his dismissal for dangerous play at Leyton Orient in September, and in the previous game – the Bristol derby – Ian Alexander was ordered off after being cautioned twice.

In October the capacity at Twerton Park was raised to almost 10,000 by the introduction of a family enclosure. Rovers were allowed to open the section behind the Bath End goal for families, pensioners, children under fifteen years of age, and women. Another 769 spaces became available in a previously unoccupied area, raising the number permitted in the ground to 9,813. The Bristol End Enclosure behind the goal was also made available for home supporters arriving at least 20 minutes before the kick-off. No fans were allowed to stand behind the new family enclosure and the exit gates into the car park at the Bath end. Gates swelled with a new record attendance of 9,813 for the league derby, which produced an average for the season of 6,209, the best for ten years and up by 17 per cent on the previous season and by a massive 91 per cent on the first year at Bath. The ground gamble had paid off.

Rovers played matches on every day of the week during the 1989/90 season. Five on Tuesday – Birmingham City at home and visits to Cardiff, Leyton Orient, Huddersfield and Reading with four on Wednesday – Bristol City, Bury, Huddersfield at Twerton Park and an away trip to Wigan. Three games took place on Sunday – all home fixtures verses Bolton, Leyton Orient and Walsall and three on Monday – away matches at Birmingham, Rotherham and Tranmere. The season also included a Thursday night visit to Notts County and a Friday trip to Crewe Alexandra. The remaining 27 games were contested on the traditional Saturday.

Gerry Francis and his staff conducted their daily business from a group of Portacabins within the grounds of Cadbury's Chocolate Factory at Keynsham which on match days involved the logistics of transporting all that was required to Twerton Park and returning it after the game. Ray Kendall's daily routine included an early morning visit to the Crest Hotel at Hambrook to pick up a box of ice for physiotherapist Roy Dolling if needed for the treatment of injured players, as there was no water supply at the training ground. On match days the ice was also required for drinks in the bar!

Defender Steve Yates, who enjoyed a fine season at the heart of the defence, was awarded three separate individual honours, being named as Young Player of the Season by Rovers' Young Pirates, Rovers' Supporters' Club and the President's Club. Ian Holloway was voted Rovers' Supporters' Club Player of the Year. In deserved recognition of his achievement in winning the Third Division title and getting to Wembley from a position of apparent weakness Gerry Francis won the Third Division Barclays Manager of the Year award. On picking up the trophy and a cheque for £1,000, Rovers' manager joked 'I'll be able to buy a player now – £1,000 – that's two players'.

# 4

# WEMBLEY

The Football League Trophy is a knockout competition open to clubs from Football League One and Football League Two. The competition was inaugurated as the Associate Members' Cup in the 1983/84 season (when League One and Two were known as Divisions Three and Four), as a way of providing more games for the lower division clubs, but from 1992 it has been named the Football League Trophy after the lower league clubs became Full Members of the league. Apart from the first year when it was not sponsored, the competition has also been known by its various past sponsorship names: the Freight Rover Trophy, the Sherpa Van Trophy, the Leyland Daf Cup, the Autoglass Trophy, the Auto Windscreens Shield, LDV Vans Trophy and since 2007 the Johnstone's Paint Trophy. The first final in 1984 was to have been played at the original Wembley, but due to damage to the pitch caused during the Horse of the Year show it was moved to Hull. From 2001 to 2007 when Wembley was being rebuilt, the Football League Trophy finals were played at the Millennium Stadium, Cardiff. The basic format of the competition since its beginnings has been to run two parallel north/south competitions, with the winners of both now meeting in the national final at the 90,000-seat Wembley Stadium.

It began on a November evening at Torquay in front of just over 2,000 spectators when Rovers faced the previous season's beaten finalists and culminated in Bristol Rovers' first ever visit in its 107-year history to the home of English football, Wembley Stadium. Rovers' big day

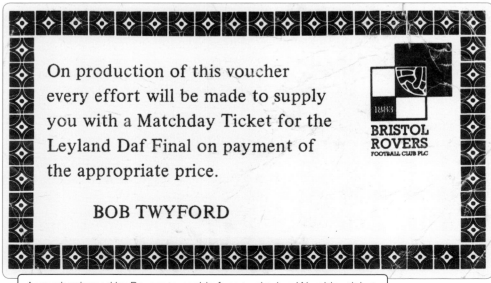

On production of this voucher every effort will be made to supply you with a Matchday Ticket for the Leyland Daf Final on payment of the appropriate price.

BOB TWYFORD

1883

BRISTOL
ROVERS
FOOTBALL CLUB PLC

A voucher issued by Rovers to enable fans to obtain a Wembley ticket.

Co-author Ian Haddrell's match day ticket for the Leyland Daf Cup Final tie.

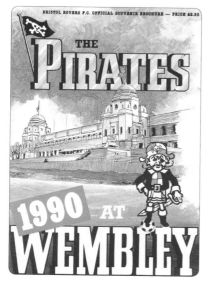

Rovers produced a commemorative brochure to mark the club's first Wembley appearance compiled by Mike Jay.

out was a party not to be missed and the 32,000-strong blue and white army in the football specials and the cavalcade of cars, vans and buses heading east from one of the smallest grounds in the Football League, were not overawed at finding themselves in the vast, historic Wembley bowl.

The final was played on the occasion of Jackie Pitt's 70th birthday. Pitt, who attended the match, made 467 league appearances for Rovers between 1946 and 1958, became groundsman at Eastville on his retirement from playing and from 1986 was groundsman at Twerton Park. After forty years of working in Second and Third Division dressing rooms, long servant Ray Kendall had this to say about the occasion, 'Just as it is every footballer's dream to play at the famous stadium, so it is every kit manager's dream to lay out the gear in the dressing room there'. Former goalkeeper Nigel Martyn was also at the game watching his ex-teammates from the commentary box providing summaries of the match for Radio Bristol.

A veterans' warm-up game in support of the National Children's Home saw Bristol Strollers and Tranmere Roamers draw 1–1, Alan Warboys and Frank Worthington scoring the goals in a match which also

Gerry Francis enjoys a snack on the Rovers team coach en route to Wembley Stadium.

featured George Best, Bobby Moore, four members of the pop group Spandau Ballet and the England rugby international Wade Dooley and which was refereed by the veteran Jack Taylor, famous for officiating in the 1974 FIFA World Cup final where he awarded two penalties during the first 30 minutes.

## Sunday 20 May 1990. Wembley Stadium. Leyland Daf Cup final

**Bristol Rovers** 1 – White
**Tranmere Rovers** 2 – Muir, Steel
**Half-time**: 0–1
**Attendance**: 48,402
**Referee**: Vic Callow (Solihull)
**Bristol Rovers**: Parkin, Alexander, Twentyman, Yates, Mehew, Jones, Holloway, Reece, White, Saunders, Purnell. Substitutes: Nixon for Alexander (44 mins), McClean for Purnell (80 mins).
**Tranmere Rovers**: Nixon, Garnett, Mungall, McNab, Hughes, Vickers, Malkin, Harvey, Steel, Muir, Thomas. Substitutes: Bishop (not used), Fairclough (not used).

Gerry Francis selected the eleven players, for Bristol Rovers' 60th match of the season (League, FA Cup, League Cup, Leyland Daf Cup and Gloucestershire FA Senior Professional Cup), who had featured most regularly in his side throughout the season. One disappointed team member was Tony Sealy (Rovers' most experienced player) forced to watch the game from the sidelines as he had not recovered from the fracture to his right leg suffered against Cardiff in March. He missed the vital run-in, as Rovers clinched the Third Division championship, and the chance for the thirty-one-year-old striker to add to his 1979 Wembley League Cup final appearance. As expected Tranmere brought in twenty-year-old former YTS product Shaun Garnett for the suspended Dave Higgins, alongside defender Mark Hughes, a former Bristol Rovers apprentice, who left the club in 1984 having made 73 league appearances for the Pirates over five seasons. On the

Front cover of the Wembley matchday programme.

substitutes bench the Birkenhead club included David Fairclough who had seven previous experiences of Wembley whilst with Liverpool, including featuring in the starting line-up of the 1978 European Cup final. Indeed, most of the Tranmere squad had been to Wembley before in the Mercantile Credit Centenary Festival in April 1988 reaching the semi-finals and only going out on penalties to eventual winners Nottingham Forest.

Rovers' army of Gasheads dominated the pre-match scenes in carnival style, while Tranmere's faithful strove hard to make themselves heard.

Immediately after the teams had been presented to guest of honour Sir Stanley Matthews, Gerry Francis disappeared down the tunnel wearing the blazer and flannels bought by the club for the entire squad, before re-emerging just before the kick-off dressed in his lucky light-grey siren suit. Kenny

Gerry Francis leads his Bristol Rovers team on to the Wembley pitch.

A contingent of 'Fellowship Gas' from Horfield amongst the large Rovers following at Wembley included: Gary Starr; Mark Tyler; Steve Harris; Martin Groves; Tony Murray; Dave Burke; Steve 'Bambi' Bennett; Simon Revill; Mark Revill.

Winger Phil Purnell sets off on an attacking run at Wembley past Tranmere's Tony Thomas.

Hibbitt, appointed Walsall's manager on 16 May, changed his mind about not attending the final and returned to take his place on the bench beside Gerry Francis. 'I played twice at Wembley in League Cup finals, but have never seen anything like that sea of blue,' said the departed Rover.

The Merseysiders, looking for revenge after being beaten twice by Rovers in the league, were quickly into their stride, Ian Muir driving in a good effort at Brian Parkin in the 3rd minute. Carl Saunders then let fly after being let in by Vickers and the Tranmere keeper Nixon flew to his left to parry the shot and then to scoop the ball away as Ian Holloway desperately tried to force the ball home. After 9 minutes Tranmere took the lead. Neil McNab's throw from the right to Mark Hughes was knocked into the box for Chris Malkin, who beat Steve Yates to nod the ball down for Ian Muir who hit a right-foot half-volley from the edge of the penalty area past the diving Parkin. It was Muir's 35th goal of the season and his seventh of the Leyland Daf run of 8 matches. Rovers' top scorer David Mehew came closest to leveling the scores before the break, shooting just over the crossbar from Devon White's flick-on in the 16th minute.

As Tranmere regained the initiative, Andy Reece was forced to clear from the six-yard box after Thomas had headed down Malkin's deep cross, then Steel shot narrowly wide from 25 yards following Thomas' right-wing cross. John King's side had the chance to increase their lead in the 38th minute when McNab put Steel through. His pass found Malkin but Steve Yates made a crucial interception. Just before the interval Ian Alexander was forced out of the game with an ankle injury, inflicted by McNab's late challenge in the centre circle, as he put Carl Saunders away. Rovers' striker eluded Nixon and was rugby-tackled in the penalty area but the whistle had already been blown for the foul on Alexander. With substitute Paul Nixon deployed in a wide midfield role, Mehew switched to partner Holloway in the centre and Reece moved into the back-four. Phil Purnell spurned a half chance late in first-half injury time, scooping the ball wide after Devon White's heavy challenge on goalkeeper Nixon.

From Paul Nixon's cross, Devon White heads downwards before collecting the rebound to score.

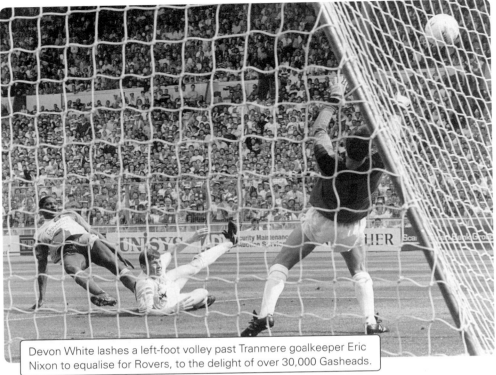

Devon White lashes a left-foot volley past Tranmere goalkeeper Eric Nixon to equalise for Rovers, to the delight of over 30,000 Gasheads.

Phil Purnell congratulates Devon White on his Wembley goal, while David Mehew shows his joy to the fans.

Striker Carl Saunders deftly knocks the ball past former Rovers defender Mark Hughes' sliding tackle.

It needed one of Gerry Francis' famous half-time team talks to improve Rovers' fortunes and whatever was said in the Wembley dressing room had the desired effect. Rovers attacked with more vigour for the first 15 minutes after the interval. First White had a header blocked by the Tranmere goalkeeper from a Holloway corner, Paul Nixon's volley was blocked in the same attack and then Eric Nixon saved from Mehew's powerful shot. Parkin was alert to keep out a Malkin header on his line at the other end. The goal Rovers had been pressing for came in the 51st minute. Mehew's long clearance out of defence was chased by Carl Saunders who fed Paul Nixon on the right. Nixon's cross eluded Mark Hughes and found Devon White on the far post, whose initial header was deflected back off Hughes and White gratefully accepted the second chance, hitting a left-foot shot on to the underside of the crossbar and down over the line. The 30,000 Gasheads present celebrated loudly.

Thirteen minutes into the second half Ian Holloway put Saunders through, only for the striker to be sent crashing to the ground by goalkeeper Eric Nixon on the edge of the penalty area. It seemed the least Rovers deserved was a free-kick, but referee Vic Callow waved

Defeated and dejected, Rovers' players applaud the massed ranks of supporters at Wembley after losing the Leyland Daf Cup Final.

play on as Saunders lay in agony. No offside was given and not surprisingly Francis was off his bench in fury at the decision, as Mr Callow awarded a goal kick. In the 70th minute Saunders curled a measured 25-yard shot wide of Eric Nixon only for the ball to hit the goalkeeper's right post and go out for a goal kick. Two minutes later, the miss became significant as Tranmere were again in front.

From a Harvey free-kick the ball was intercepted by Steve Yates, but he lost possession in his own penalty area after a determined challenge by Mark Hughes and the ball fell for Ian Muir in space. He spotted Jim Steel on the far post and his cleverly flighted right-wing cross allowed the striker the simplest of headers to beat Brian Parkin from 3 yards, with Rovers' players claiming Steel had pushed Twentyman in order to get to the ball. Rovers had produced so many comebacks on their run to the Championship, and came to Wembley with a run of only one defeat in 27 matches, but this time it was not to be. In a brave final effort during the 3 minutes of injury time, White failed to get in a strike after Paul Nixon's persistence won the ball on the byline, then Saunders saw an overhead kick float wide of the far post and had a well-struck shot saved by Eric Nixon.

Rovers' fans, who outnumbered their Tranmere counterparts by two to one, were stunned into silence as celebrations began at the other end of the stadium at the final whistle. For

Captain Vaughan Jones leads his side past the blue and white sea of Rovers fans on their way back to the Wembley dressing room.

Phil Purnell's Leyland Daf Cup Wembley medal.

the players, so eager to have something to celebrate after their first appearance beneath the famous twin towers, it was worse. The bodies stretched out on the hallowed turf as the final whistle blew said it all. A mixture of dejection and exhaustion made it so difficult to put on a brave face. Francis, finishing as a Wembley loser for the first time in his career, chivvied and cajoled his despondent men into acknowledging their supporters before the cup and medals presentations. There was a chorus of 'Goodnight Irene' but one lacking the gusto of earlier renditions. The losing side went up first to receive their medals, injured Ian Alexander painfully bringing up the rear, at the end of what had been a gripping final. Rovers' pedestrian lap of honour brought affectionate and sympathetic applause from their own followers and a sportingly generous ovation when they passed the Tranmere section of the ground. Tranmere returned to Wembley the following weekend to contest a Second Division place with Notts County in the Third Division play-off final and were beaten 2–0.

Captain Vaughan Jones threw his loser's medal away incensed with some of the decisions made by referee Vic Callow, which Jones believed cost Rovers the match. However, Devon White picked it up and handed it back to the disappointed Welshman afterwards. Jones, denied the glory of holding the cup aloft at Wembley in his testimonial season, summed up the occasion:

One of the proudest moments of the day was seeing thousands of Rovers fans streaming up Wembley Way two hours before kick-off. The disappointment of the result will be overshadowed in the long term by memories of being the first captain to lead out Rovers at Wembley.

A disappointing end to the season for the Gasheads but, nonetheless, it was a major achievement for a club of the stature of Bristol Rovers to reach a Wembley final. The season had brought much greater success than any realistic Rovers fan could have dreamed of and as there had been many lean years for Bristol Rovers, the season's euphoria of promotion and the first appearance at Wembley was understandable. After all, it acknowledges what is unarguably the most triumphant season in the club's history.

# 5

# BRIEF STAY IN DIVISION TWO

Rovers' long-awaited return to Division Two was somewhat overshadowed by events off the field. The continued search for a stadium nearer Rovers' fan base in East Bristol was still encountering problems. With the proposed move to Stoke Gifford rejected, much emphasis was placed on a potential move to Mangotsfield. With the success of the previous season, the club now seemed more likely to interest the local authorities, but in September 1990 the plans for a stadium at Carsons Road, Mangotsfield were rejected. A week later in the early hours of 16 September, a serious fire damaged the Main Stand at Twerton Park.

Immediately after the Wembley final speculation began as to whether Gerry Francis would stay with the club or opt for a fresh challenge. The *Bristol Evening Post* suggested that French club Paris St Germain and Spanish First Division club Logrones were ready to step in when the manager's contract expired in mid-June. His exploits with Rovers had attracted national acclaim and several chairmen had cast covetous eyes towards him, so it came as a great relief to all Rovers supporters when, on Friday 15 June, Francis signed a new one-year contract to end all speculation about his immediate future. However, a week after he had signed the contract,

In September 1990, the Main Stand at Twerton Park was severely damaged by an arson attack.

Rovers were contacted by Aston Villa who wanted Francis to take over from Graham Taylor; he had left to become the new manager of England. But their approach was turned down by the Rovers board who refused Villa chairman Doug Ellis permission to speak to Francis. Despite being disappointed that he never had the chance to talk to a big club like Aston Villa, Francis ,who had always preached honesty and integrity to his players, honoured his contract with Rovers. Apart from the departure of Peter Cawley and the arrival of £10,000 winger Tony Pounder from Weymouth, it was largely the championship-winning side that attained a respectable mid-table position, with Rovers' financial position virtually necessitating a return to the 'no buy, no sell' policy of the early post-war years at Eastville. Although, when the players reported back from pre-season training Vaughan Jones requested a pay rise, but he was told that he could not have what he was asking for and was promptly put on the transfer list.

The opening fixture of the 1990/91 season was a visit to Filbert Street, where Rovers were narrowly defeated 3–2 by Leicester City; captain Vaughan Jones scoring the club's first goal back in Division Two. This was followed by a 2–1 victory at home to Charlton Athletic, with Mehew and White scoring for the Pirates in front of 5,000 fans. On a Wednesday night in September, Blackburn Rovers recorded a 2–1 victory at Twerton Park; ending the Pirates' proud run of 34 home league games unbeaten. Three days later, Sheffield Wednesday also won at 'Fortress Twerton'. On 6 October Rovers avoided dropping into the relegation zone – reorganisation having meant only two clubs would be relegated – due to the 3 second-half goals Oxford United conceded at Barnsley. However, by the first week in December Rovers lay in 9th place in the table, the highest place in an encouraging season. As the season wore on Gerry Francis recalled Ian Willmott briefly, and Billy Clark who, after many substitute appearances and missing the entire promotion season through injury, played in his first games since October 1988.

Adrian Boothroyd and Gavin Kelly both broke into the league side, and two years on, Dennis Bailey enjoyed a second, if less prolific, loan spell with the Pirates. Once again, relative success was achieved with a consistently settled side. Twentyman, Holloway and Reece were ever-presents, but in truth the team virtually picked itself for much of the season. Carl Saunders, after enjoying a mid-season purple patch of 9 goals in 10 league matches, finished the season as the club's top goalscorer with 16 goals in league action. The all-conquering side of 1989/90 understandably found the going considerably harder in the higher division, but a final placing of 13th, the club's highest since 1959/60, was commendable. Following just two league substitute appearances during 1990/91 Christian McClean was finally granted a transfer after numerous requests, and left for Swansea in the summer of 1991, his final appearance being when he replaced Tony Pounder in the 1–0 home defeat to Sheffield Wednesday in October 1990. Tony Sealy and Paul Nixon both departed for foreign fields during the season, having made only a handful of appearances in Division Two. Sealy moved to Finland whilst Nixon took up an offer in March to play in Hong Kong. However, an altogether more significant departure during the close season was that of Gerry Francis, whose success at Rovers on a shoestring budget was bound to lead to further interest from larger clubs. His year-long contract up, Francis left Rovers shortly after the end of the 1990/91 season to become manager of First Division Queens Park Rangers.

During his first stint as Rovers' boss the popular Francis gained a reputation for astute financial management and for spotting potential in unknown players. His skills as a coach were apparent and he was able to spot latent talent which he quickly exploited, largely signing unknowns with non-League backgrounds and discards to add to Rovers' limited experience. According to Roy Dolling, Francis had a 'fascinating style of management' and was quoted as saying with regard to one particularly inept first-half performance, 'what I said to them at half-time would be unprintable on the radio.' When Francis joined Rovers he stated that he would stay for three years, but the club were fortunate in having such an outstanding coach for an extra season and no one should belittle what Gerry Francis did for Rovers. To get them out of the Third Division and to a showpiece final with the slender resources he had to work with was a superb achievement. He was proud that Bristol Rovers under his management never lost 2 consecutive matches during the 1988/89 and 1989/90 seasons. The following table shows Francis' record as manager.

| Competition | P | W | D | L | F | A | Pts |
|---|---|---|---|---|---|---|---|
| Football League | 184 | 78 | 57 | 49 | 262 | 201 | 291 |
| FA Cup | 10 | 3 | 3 | 4 | 18 | 10 | |
| League Cup | 8 | 2 | 2 | 4 | 4 | 8 | |
| Gloucestershire FA Cup | 5 | 2 | 0 | 3 | 8 | 11 | |
| Zenith Data Systems Cup | 2 | 1 | 0 | 1 | 3 | 3 | |

Ian Holloway quickly followed Francis to London in a £230,000 deal, having unknowingly made the last appearance of his second spell with Rovers in the 1–1 home draw with West Bromwich Albion in the final game of the season.

The Rovers board moved quickly to find a replacement for Francis appointing Martin Dobson, an erstwhile classy midfielder with Burnley, Everton and England, who was just weeks into his job as Northwich Victoria manager. Geoff Twentyman applied for the vacant manager's job, but was disappointed not to have been given the opportunity to manage the club. Dobson was able to call upon the services of two experienced signings in Fulham's Justin Skinner and Derby County's Steve Cross, and in starting the season temporarily without the suspended Carl Saunders, Dobson gave career starts to Lee Maddison, Gareth Taylor and Marcus Stewart. Yet Dobson's side were defeated in six of its first 9 league matches and with the side languishing at the foot of the table at the beginning of October the manager's brief tenure was over. The one victory, 2–1 at home to Oxford United, marked the first game of the season for captain Vaughan Jones who had been injured in the summer. However, his return lasted all of 60 seconds before he suffered a broken leg that ruled him out for a further 14 months. Coach Dennis Rofe took over as caretaker-manager and was elevated to the post of manager on 10 January 1992. Rovers' nadir that season came at the Abbey Stadium in February when Cambridge United inflicted Rovers' worst defeat since February 1987, with a 6–1 victory. One of Cambridge's goalscorers was substitute John Taylor who, despite his goal, had been struggling to score regularly for the U's and within weeks Taylor was a Rovers player. A revival by Rofe's side from January saw them rise to and consolidate a mid-table position finishing the season in 13th spot.

The highlight, however, for players and supporters alike were the two Fourth Round FA Cup ties against a Liverpool side that had finished runners-up in Division One the previous season. A ground record all-ticket crowd of 9,484 watched a thrilling 1-1 draw at Twerton Park with Carl Saunders' equalising goal earning a replay at Anfield. Extraordinarily, Saunders' long-

Carl Saunders, out of picture, scores past Liverpool goalkeeper Bruce Grobbelaar to put Rovers one up in the FA Cup tie in front of the record attendance at Twerton Park.

range right-foot volley in front of the Kop gave Rovers an interval lead, but before a 30,142 crowd Liverpool won through with 2 second-half goals and progressed to beat Sunderland in the Final.

The 0–0 home draw with Barnsley on 21 March 1992 saw the final appearance of two of Rovers' 1990 Wembley side when Devon White and Phil Purnell pulled on the blue and white quarters for the last time. White left for Cambridge United that month in a £100,000 plus John Taylor swap deal and then rejoined former boss Gerry Francis at QPR the following season, whilst Purnell, loaned to Swansea City for a month in December 1991, suffered a broken leg whilst playing for Rovers reserves in April 1992 which necessitated retirement from the game twelve months later. Ian Willmott also played his last game for the Pirates against Newcastle in the opening month of the season and returned to non-League football, and Ian Hazel's final appearance on the Rovers team-sheet was as an unused substitute for the 2–2 draw at Tranmere Rovers in August 1991.

Rovers' manager Dennis Rofe returns to the Anfield dressing room after the 2–1 FA Cup Fourth Round replay defeat.

Rovers began the new season in Division One, not through any miracle of close season promotion, but due to the creation of the Premier League and the renaming of the three remaining Football League divisions as Divisions One, Two and Three. The side bore a strong resemblance to that which had finished mid-table in 1991/92, with attacking options looking exciting as John Taylor, Marcus Stewart and Carl Saunders competed for places. Goalscoring was not a problem as 55 league goals were scored during the season; the real problem in 1992/93 was the frequency of league defeats. In the first home game of the campaign against Swindon Town, having previously been unbeaten in 16 matches at Twerton Park, Rovers conceded 4 goals for the first time on that ground. On the 3 November, Rovers lost 5–1 at home to Barnsley, the heaviest home defeat since December 1976, followed by a 5–1 defeat at Wolverhampton Wanderers, conceding 5 goals in consecutive games for only the second time in the club's league history, leaving the Pirates anchored to the bottom of the table. With only two wins from 16 league matches, Dennis Rofe's traumatic start to the season was brought to end on the 9th of November to be replaced the following day by the larger-than-life Malcolm Allison. Initially, Allison's arrival instigated a change in Rovers' fortunes as a run of four straight victories without conceding a goal, including a 4–0 triumph against Bristol City in December 1992, offered fresh hope. However, by the time 'Big Mal' left in February Rovers were back in the relegation places. Coach Steve Cross took temporary charge for 3 games, prior to the appointment of John Ward on 20 March, but it was too late to prevent the inevitable relegation. Rovers lost a club record 25 league games in being relegated and the total of 11 home defeats equalled the tally set in 1947/48. The last season to date for Rovers in the second tier of English football saw final appearances by two stalwarts from the championship-winning side and Rovers' first-ever visit to Wembley as Geoff Twentyman and Vaughan Jones left the club. Twentyman after 252 league games and 6 goals moved to Yate Town in February having made his last Rovers appearance at Watford in October 1992. Former captain Jones played his 370th and final league game for the Pirates in the 1–1 home draw with Wolverhampton Wanderers on 13 March 1993 before moving to Bath City and with that the last playing link with Eastville was gone.

# 6

# 'RAGBAG ROVERS'
## THEN & NOW

Ian Alexander returned to his native Scotland, works for the Glasgow Regeneration Agency.

Marcus Browning dons a Rovers shirt once more for a charity match at the Memorial Ground, 2 May 2011.

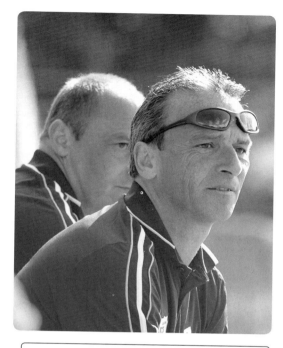

David Byrne left Swindon Town in August 2010 after four years with the Robins.

SPALL

Pete Cawley takes to the field at Layer Road before a Colchester Legends match in 2010.

Ian Hazel joined Carshalton Athletic's management team in 2008.

Ian Holloway at Bristol Rovers' 125th anniversary dinner, April 2009.

Vaughan Jones at the Memorial
Stadium on 2 May 2011.

Nigel Martyn outside of the Memorial
Stadium, May 2012, prior to a charity
match – his first game for six years.

Christian McClean made an appearance for Boxted Lodgers in October 2011.

David Mehew, pictured in 2011, became manager of Southern League Premier side Gloucester City in 2008.

Paul Nixon at Claudelands Rovers Junior FC prizegiving, Galloway Park, Hamilton, New Zealand, 23 September 2011.

Brian Parkin, photographed in July 2011, is now a taxi driver in Bath.

Gary Penrice outside his South Gloucestershire home, June 2011.

Phil Purnell still makes regular appearances for Winterbourne Cricket Club First XI.

Andy Reece played for the Rovers Legends side against Bristol City Legends, 2 May 2011.

Carl Saunders promoting Bristol Trates, a community task force for grassroots football in Bristol.

Tony Sealy, pictured in June 2011, is Director of Operations at Hong Kong FC.

Geoff Twentyman, sports editor and presenter on Radio Bristol, photographed at the Memorial Stadium in May 2011.

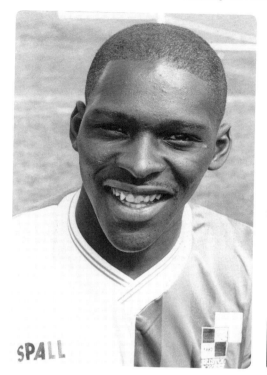

Devon White returned to Radford FC in July 2008 to officially launch the Supporters' Club and open the new club shop.

Ian Willmott, photographed in 2011, works as an accounts manager for a South Bristol roofing company.

Steve Yates moved to the Greek island of Crete after retiring from football.

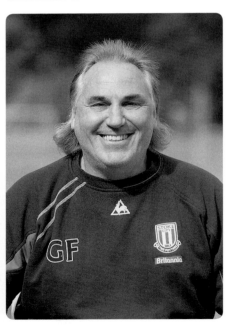

Gerry Francis, still involved in football coaching at Stoke City.

Kenny Hibbitt has been employed by the Premier League since 2003 as a Match Delegate.

If you enjoyed this book, you may also be interested in…

## A Season to Remember: Bristol Rovers' Promotion Season 1973/74

MICHAEL JAY AND IAN HADDRELL

In the 1973/74 season, Bristol Rovers clinched promotion to the old 'Second Division' in one of the club's most memorable campaigns. The side went unbeaten for thirty-two games, setting a new club record. Anyone who witnessed this exciting period in the club's history will enjoy reliving some of the magic through the memories and images collected here, while all those fans who are too young to remember it can gain some idea of just what made this season so special.

978 0 7524 5832 8

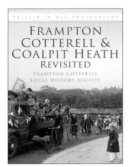

## Frampton Cotterell and Coalpit Heath Revisited

FRAMPTON COTTERELL LOCAL HISTORY SOCIETY & IAN HADDRELL

This fascinating new collection of over 200 archive images compiled by the Frampton Cotterell and District Local History Society, provides a unique insight into the everyday life of the people who have lived, worked and played in the area between the late Victorian era and the 1980s. Each image is accompanied by an informative caption, bringing the past to life and describing how it once was in these former coal mining communities. This pictorial history is sure to delight locals and visitors alike.

978 0 7524 6469 5

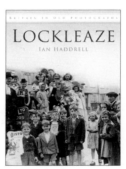

## Lockleaze: In Old Photographs

IAN HADDRELL

This captivating book illustrating Lockleaze contains over 200 rare and, in many cases, unpublished images that explore the social history of this close-knit area of Bristol. Compiled using residents' photographs and archive material, this collection recalls the people, places and events that have shaped Lockleaze's past. Produced by the author of Lockleaze Schools, informative captions compliment the images to reveal the story of how the neighbourhood has developed in the post-war era.

978 0 7524 5407 8

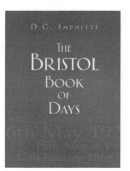

## The Bristol Book of Days

D. G. AMPHLETT

Taking you through the year day by day, The Bristol Book of Days contains a quirky, eccentric, amusing or important event or fact from different periods of history, many of which had a major impact on the religious and political history of England as a whole. Ideal for dipping into, this addictive little book will keep you entertained and informed. Featuring hundreds of snippets of information gleaned from the vaults of Bristol's archives, it will delight residents and visitors alike.

978 0 7524 6038 3

Visit our website and discover thousands of other History Press books.

**www.thehistorypress.co.uk**

The History Press